POLICE STRIKE – 1919

By the same author

NON-FICTION

Atlantis
The Warring Seas
Black Avalanche (with Mary Sellwood)
Stand By To Die
HMS Electra (in collaboration with Lieut. Cmdr T. J. Cain)
The Saturday Night Soldiers
The Damned Don't Drown
The Red-Gold Flame

FICTION

Children Of The Damned
Too Hot To Handle

POLICE STRIKE–1919

A. V. Sellwood

W. H. ALLEN · LONDON

A Howard & Wyndham Company
1978

Photoset, printed and bound in Great Britain by
REDWOOD BURN LIMITED, Trowbridge & Esher
for the Publishers, W. H. Allen & Co. Ltd, 44 Hill Street
London W1X 8LB

ISBN 0 491 02153 4

Contents

On a Personal Note . . .

For kindly providing me with their personal recollections of the events leading up to the Police Strike of 1919 and the tragic events that followed it my particular thanks are due to Messrs Leonard Petchey, Richard O'Keeffe, A. ('Shiny') Salt and Tom O'Brien, all of them former members of the Liverpool City Police Force.

My thanks are also due to Mr Douglas Massey, himself a former police officer, for lending me, and permitting me to quote from, his thesis on the Strike for the Ethel Wormald College of Education; to Mr Frank Harris BSc, Head of the College's History (Special Studies) Department; the Liverpool City Police Comrades' Association for their introductions and advice, and to *Service*, journal of the Association, for permission to publish material based on a contribution from ex-Sergeant 26 'A' John Ford.

I am also indebted to the Public Records Office, the Metropolitan Police Force, the Police Federation, the *Daily Mirror* Library, for help in my researches, and Mirror Group Newspapers for granting access to the files of both the *Daily Mirror* and the *Daily Herald* of the time.

The picture of London strikers returning their uniforms to their police station is reproduced by courtesy of the London Borough of Tower Hamlets Amenities Committee; *Liverpool Daily Post and Echo* kindly provided the pictures of the Liverpool street scene, taken the morning after the riots, while the *Daily Mirror* supplied the close-up pictures of the shops those riots had shattered.

Out of the Blue

A battleship dropping anchor off a British city to overcome rebellion in the docks . . . soldiers, with bayonets fixed, advancing slowly through the city's slums beneath a hail of missiles from a pillaging mob . . . tanks clattering noisily through the shattered shopping centre with orders to 'secure' the civic buildings and the main railway station . . . to stunned observers it did not seem possible that this could be happening in Britain. All this, and not a policeman in sight.

Yet such was the scene in Liverpool on August Bank Holiday 1919. It was one that was duplicated in nearby Bootle and Birkenhead. A tragedy that also had repercussions on the streets of London and Birmingham.

The Law had seen red. The police had gone on strike. And police and public alike were paying dearly for the consequences. With the policemen off the beat, the mobs were running riot.

In the windows of the looted shops and houses along one of Birkenhead's main thoroughfares not a pane of glass remained intact. A magistrate, reading the Riot Act to the mixed community of Liverpool 5 – racked by bitter racial and sectarian hatreds – was forced to shelter in the turret of an armoured car. And, down in London, there was the incredible spectacle of policemen fighting savagely with policemen.

Except by a few people – their ranks thinning every year – who personally experienced the violence that followed the withdrawal of the traditional guardians of the public, the Police Strike of 1919 is forgotten, or else casually dismissed as an attempt at industrial action that mercifully failed.

However, it was one for which the strikers paid an appallingly

1

heavy price.

In Liverpool's Rose Hill police station, as in practically every other police station in the city's thirty-three mile circumference, a shapeless mound of discarded blue uniforms and helmets grew larger every hour. Several of the cast-off tunics carried the bright splash of medal ribbons above their left breast pockets: Long Service; Good Conduct; Personal Gallantry. Like the careers and livelihood of those who had proudly worn them, tunics and ribbons lay ingloriously in the dust.

Described to me by one of the PCs who remained loyal throughout the strike, the sad scene in Rose Hill was duplicated in police stations throughout the country.

Every one of the 955 Liverpool policemen who had 'come out' to secure recognition of their Union, threatened with extinction by the Government's Police Bill, had been dismissed.

In London, over a thousand of their colleagues in the Metropolitan Police Force shared their fate.

There were similar sackings in the City of London Police, in the Birmingham City Police, and in the police forces of Birkenhead and Bootle.

For a variety of reasons, which will emerge in the course of this book, nearly 97 per cent of the country's policemen had refused to follow the strike call.

Yet the civil disturbances that had arisen from even a limited response to strike had been so great that a harsh deterrent was deemed essential to prevent worse troubles for the future. Authority had been flouted, and had struck back hard: but whether its apportionment of penalty and blame was equitable – or even wise – is debatable.

In the period that immediately followed the Strike's destructive course, and the backlash that cost 2,300 policemen their careers and reputations – not one of the men was ever reinstated – few asked how the friendly and trusted 'bobbies' had come to be labelled 'red', and even 'bolshevik' by certain elements in

Parliament and the Press.

Few politicians or senior civil servants cared to look inward at the time, and ponder on how much *their* attitudes and policies could have led men with such high traditions of discipline and service into taking a step so fantastically out of character.

And perhaps even fewer of the trade union militants who had urged them to take that step cared to remember how little support, except for lip service, had been forthcoming for the 'police brothers' when the crisis had exploded, leaving them among its victims.

Appalled by the eruption of the underworld on to the streets, the country at large was in no mood to look any further for scapegoats beyond the strikers themselves. Yet scapegoats there were in plenty, had anyone cared to look . . . a Prime Minister, promising one thing to the discontented police rank-and-file, but meaning quite another; a Government long accustomed to singling out the police service as easy victim for its cuts in public spending; a bureaucracy accustomed for decades to keeping the PC at the end of the pay queue: and left wing militants, eager to exploit their old enemies' discontent and bring them under the control of the TUC . . . while the strikers were the ones to suffer for the 'mutiny'; here at least, it might be felt, were accessories to the act, and the combined effects of all of them provided a frightening warning for the future.

Fifty-nine years have passed since the time when the law saw red, but the causes that led to Liverpool's ordeal in 1919 can now be found, on an even bigger scale, in every major British city.

They included, and still include, a mixed community, of many national origins, living in poverty, alienated from the majority, and frequently at war within itself: an administrative machine that each year becomes more remote from those it was created to serve; a powerful minority of criminals, playing for higher stakes than ever before; and the growing cult of violence for violence's sake . . . the mixture is highly explosive; those who might be able to defuse it are short on the ground.

We may, all of us, feel concerned as to what will happen to our country and its system should the overworked men on the beat,

3

discouraged by lack of support from Parliament and the courts, and desperately underprivileged as regards pay and working conditions, decide they must 'see red' – or even blue – tomorrow.

A. V. Sellwood
Seaford, Sussex

CHAPTER ONE

Word of a Wizard

'Lloyd George knew my Father
My Father knew Lloyd George . . .'

Sung to the tune of 'Onward Christian Soldiers' by a vast procession of policemen – all of them out of uniform – carrying un-
likely-looking placards of protest and complaint, this slanderous
ditty from the trenches on how best to get promotion and a cushy
billet was one of several, equally irreverent, to echo through
Whitehall.

It was a hot and dusty Saturday afternoon, the last day of
August 1918, but the mood of the marchers, in contrast to their
slogans, was good humoured and relaxed, as befitted London
'bobbies' even in their present, most unexpected role.

'Lloyd George knew my Father,
My Father knew Lloyd George . . .'

At the head of the procession, and joining in the chorus was
Police Constable Jim Marston, heavy-framed, thick-
moustached, a leader flushed with success and the applause of
his colleagues. And if 'our Jim', as he was popularly known,
should be feeling that the words had a special – and cheering –
significance for himself and his fortunes in politics there were
many who would have thought it understandable.

Not that Marston Senior, tough old Norfolk countryman, had
even exchanged as much as a nod or a syllable with the great war
leader; indeed to judge by the radical causes espoused by the
Marston family, he would not even have given him the benefit of

his vote. Nor was Marston Junior – as even his enemies would agree – one whose ambitions were centred on acquiring a cushy billet.

A fiery militant in Labour's cause, a plinth in some Hall of Socialist Heroes would – so they said – have had far greater appeal for him. But, as from now, Jim Marston 'knew', or thought he did, Lloyd George. And, even more important, Lloyd George now knew Jim Marston. Agreement had been reached between the two, and the fight for a police union could be considered as good as won.

Less than thirty-six hours had passed since Marston had dared to do the thing that, until then, had been dismissed as 'quite unthinkable'; the 'unthinkable' act that had given him, if not a plinth, at least a niche in history.

He had called on the men of the Metropolitan Police Force to take strike action, classed by statute as unlawful, and labelled mutiny by the Home Office. More, he had made that call as chairman of the National Union of Police and Prison Officers, a 'union' the Government had refused to recognise, and to which police and prison officers were forbidden to belong. Even to Marston, the response had been astounding.

It had been the first large-scale strike in the history of the British police; one that had taken the authorities, and over eight million Londoners, completely by surprise. It had been a strike that had carried with it every police district in the capital, only two days after a meeting of superintendents had reported that the force had no complaints, and all was well. And it had been a strike that, following the personal intervention of Lloyd George, had now ended in total victory for the strikers; or so it seemed. A settlement concluded in Number Ten in which Marston and his colleagues, to the evident annoyance of both Commissioner and Home Secretary, had come off best: one in which – almost – their every demand had been met.

'Now don't forget,' the Prime Minister had said as, shaking hands with Marston, he bade the delegates goodbye, 'if ever a similar situation should arise you must come and see me.'

Marston would not forget. Here indeed, was a moment to

savour. It was not every day that a union damned as 'illegal' could look to a Prime Minister as ally!

The Premier had been told that the new proposals would have to be put before the strikers at a rally on Tower Hill, but this was for the sake of form alone: not for one moment had there been any serious fear of their rejection. In fact, when Marston and James Carmichael, left-wing leader of the London Trades Council, mounted the rostrum to advise the members to accept, they had to yell at them to make themselves heard above the handclaps and the cheering.

Though underpaid, over-disciplined and overworked, for men with such a long tradition of service to the public and loyalty to the State, the strike decision had been a difficult one to make, and there was relief at the conflict's ending, as well as elation at victory.

The reinstatement of PC Tommy Thiel, dismissed for belonging to the Union; an increase of pensionable pay, an increase of war bonus, the provision of widows' pensions and the right to a pension at the end of twenty-six years' service: every one of these points had been conceded in the course of the talks at Number Ten.

And also agreed had been 'the establishment of an authorised organisation' to represent the men who, hitherto had no right of access to the authorities and no machinery for the discussion of their grievances.

So what more could they ask? Had they not got everything? Including, as it did, the lifting of all sanctions against those wishing to join the Union, so long as no attempt was made to interfere with the discipline of the service, the settlement indeed appeared, to quote Carmichael, 'the biggest victory for freedom and justice ever won,' and yet . . . and yet . . .

As the delegates announced their own acceptance of the terms and put them to a show of hands, which shot up as thick as a forest, there stirred among the cheers one small whisper of unease.

One of the key demands put forward during the Strike had

been recognition of the Union that had made it possible, but the settlement had merely promised 'the establishment of an *organisation* to represent the men.'

Why, it was asked, should this have been deemed necessary? Why, with the Union so very much 'established' that they were celebrating victory instead of suffering their dismissal should the Union not be accepted as 'representative' of their views?

The answer, almost unheard by the mass of the rally, was that NUPPO, as such, could not be recognised in wartime, but after the war it would be a different story.

Meanwhile, the Prime Minister, by receiving its Executive, had in fact given the Union the recognition it required, barring only the form of words.

And furthermore, Mr Lloyd George had also agreed that the Union Executive, meeting with representatives of the Home Office, should draw up the rules that would govern the new organisation. In short, as the present Executive members could be elected to the PM's brain-child, that organisation would be merely the Union under an officially acceptable name, 'dealing [Carmichael again] with every grievance you have got.'

With this, the critics had to be content, and happily the crowd dispersed, many returning to their stations for duty, and being applauded by the citizens on their way. The Union, it was agreed, had won the day, regardless of the wording of its 'recognition'.

'In fact,' one of the men was later to recall, 'the issue, at that time, was seen as a purely minor irritant, a gnat's bite on an elephant's broad back.'

Unfortunately, that irritation was to grow, and with it an infection that would spread to both trunk and tail. It was one that would finally affect the brain and, in the end, make the animal run amok.

If it had not been for the man they called the Welsh Wizard falling for his own verbal magic in effecting the 1918 'settlement', and saying one thing while meaning quite another, the National Police Strike of 1919, slightly less than a year later, and all its appalling consequences, both to the public and to the police themselves, might never have happened. As things turned out, however, the goodwill engendered by his intervention was to be all too quickly dissipated in disillusion and distrust. To many, the Wizard's wand would appear a little 'bent'.

Yet before Lloyd George's invitation to its principals the possible implications of the Strike looked threatening enough to justify unorthodox attempts to reach a solution.

With panic in Whitehall – the Guards had been sent, with machine guns, to guard Downing Street! – new crises over the Western Front and Ireland, and news to hand of fresh Bolshevik successes, the Prime Minister's magic had to be spread fairly thinly. In his effort to get rid of the problem – the police problem that was literally on his doorstep – he could perhaps be forgiven for being a trifle careless about the small print that was to be appended to the 'settlement'. He was endeavouring to meet circumstances that were not only exceptional but unique.

On Friday, the first day of the Strike, Basil Thomson, head of the CID, had to make his way to his office at Scotland Yard through a mob of strikers in plain clothes, filling the approaches to the Yard, shouting and booing.

Later, he had watched a crowd of several thousands march to Smith Square, where they were joined by other contingents from an area covering Greater London within a radius of fifteen miles from Charing Cross.

'As they crossed Old Palace Yard on their way,' he later wrote, 'they hooted and jeered at a few officers of the Special Constabulary, calling them "scabs" and "blacklegs".'

But if the attitude of his men came as an unpleasant surprise to Sir Basil, accustomed though he was to 'taking the rough with the smooth' – the effect on the more sheltered denizens of Whitehall was that of traumatic shock.

While the discussion with the strike leaders was under way, the songs of the strikers thronging the streets outside had been heard in every corner of Number Ten, a choral background severely deflating arguments in favour of a firm stand.

In addition, accurate or not, the rumour was spreading that

troops sent to take over police duties in guarding the Treasury building were fraternising with the strikers, and pledging that they would never act against them.

Add to this a slightly scandalised report in *The Times* on how, as the strikers marched through the City to Tower Hill, 'the stockbrokers and their office staffs treated them to a good-tempered cheer', and Lloyd George may well have reflected that 'to stand firm' in this particular instance was a stance more befitting a King Canute than a statesman whose reputation had been one of super-sensitivity towards the popular tide.

Mouthpiece of the diehard Tories, the *Morning Post* might fulminate – and did – about 'deserters' and 'mutiny' and hint darkly at alien influences at work, but it was hard for a community that for decades had been accustomed to trust and turn to its local 'bobbies' to believe they had been changed into bolsheviks overnight.

Again, the Prime Minister was genuinely aggrieved at the way in which, as he put it, he had been 'kept in ignorance' of the police unrest. Over the past three years parliamentary questions designed to draw attention to the hardships suffered by policemen as the result of the Government's imposed 'freeze' – which had left them a shade worse off than the lowest-paid, unskilled labourer – had been parried by reflections on 'the need to make wartime sacrifices'. All allegations of discontent within the service had been met by the Home Office's bland assurance that, apart from a radical minority, police morale had never been better. The Welsh Wizard had been badly let down by his crystal-gazers.

All the same, it was in self-congratulatory mood that he summarised the results of his meeting with the 'representatives of the policemen', and if there was a difference between that title and 'members of the Union Executive' he did not appear to worry overmuch about it, let alone consider that it might be an insurmountable difficulty in future relations between police and Government.

The police representatives had come into Number Ten like angry lions and had gone out – if not as lambs – at least with expressions of goodwill, and a feeling of satisfaction that justice, even if overdue, was being granted them. He had captivated even the fiery near-Marxist Marston and that shrewd industrial bargainer James Carmichael, with the charm that was at once his speciality and camouflage. And, best thing of all about the settlement, the extra cost would be only slightly more than what the Treasury had resigned itself to spending anyway.

Unknown to the men who were so rapturously to applaud their leaders for making Lloyd George see the light, and force the police paymasters to open up their coffers, a scheme to improve pay and pensions, and provide widows' pensions too, had already been prepared by the Commissioner, the much-maligned Sir Edward Henry. But, characteristically, he had not thought fit to discuss this with his subordinates and its progress had been delayed while the Treasury argued against his demand to include pensions for existing widows.

In fact, although Lloyd George was to get the credit for the deal – 'The Prime Minister is on our side,' claimed Marston – the scheme presented to the men was fundamentally Henry's, with the exception that it left out the existing widows.

Nor did the PM feel that his handling of the recognition issue had been anything else but skilful. He had said – had he not? – that a police union could not be recognised in wartime, when the idea might spread to the army, as it had in afflicted Russia: but he had offered the delegates an alternative method of bringing their grievances to light, and this they had accepted. By and large, all had turned out very well.

With that essential attribute to success in politics, the capacity for being all things to all men, David Lloyd George had been endowed in blessed abundance. Unfortunately, in the quest for a quick agreement he had deceived not only his audience but himself as well.

'The effect of Mr Lloyd George's reception of the Executive Committee of the Police Union is Government recognition of the Union . . .'

In his victory address to the strikers on Tower Hill that

veteran of industrial disputes, James Carmichael, had made it abundantly clear that both he and the Union leadership regarded NUPPO as having already obtained *de facto* recognition – with *de jure* to follow after the war – and had also argued that the new consultative machinery would be largely controlled by the Union, though under a different label.

And already, as though anticipating this interpretation of the conference, Sir George Cave, as Home Secretary, had rushed out a corrective statement, which he read to waiting journalists from the steps of Number Ten.

'The Prime Minister said to the deputation of policemen that he could not in wartime sanction recognition of a police union,' said Sir George who, together with the Commissioner had been present throughout the conference.

And then, having confirmed the PM's promise of 'an authorised organisation' for the men, he took pains to add, 'of course, this is quite a different thing from a union in the ordinary sense.'

A *Daily Mirror* reporter, comparing this with Carmichael's claim that the organisation 'would be formed upon your Union' was quick to note what he called, with some understatement, 'the different view' expressed by Cave. It was a difference that was temporarily lost sight of in the general relief at the ending of the Strike.

Was the whole thing a deliberate attempt by the Union leaders to add to the spoils of victory, and enhance their own prestige? A typically wily manoeuvre by Lloyd George, playing for time? It could have been either, or perhaps a bit of both, a tacit agreement by both sides to gloss over the fine print of their agreement and interpret it in terms that kept their respective supporters happy. Or it could have been a perfectly honest misunderstanding arising from the occasion's super-tension and the improvised and rushed attempts to ease it. Even now the facts are too scarce to reach a positive verdict.

To the layman it may seem strange that no shorthand writer was present at a conference convened for such a momentous issue as the restoration of police protection to the capital. It is even stranger that no official record of the proceedings – agreed by both sides – was made available to the public. For information on the ambiguities surrounding the snap settlement, there are only the fallible memories of those personally involved in the conference, and these vary widely and are often contradictory.

But one man at least had no doubts about where the major source of future discord lay, and later recorded: 'The Prime Minister's terminology about not sanctioning a union in wartime was naturally seized upon by the men as an excuse to demand recognition of the Union when peace came . . .'

In delivering this judgement, Lieutenant General Sir Nevil Macready was expressing more than the fashionable soldier-like contempt for the equivocations and weakness of the 'frocks' – the frock-coated politicians and senior civil servants. He was registering an opinion firmly based on his own experience when obliged to face the consequences of the settlement's unresolved ambiguities.

Commanding the troops drafted to South Wales during the mining crisis of 1911 – from where he derived his bogeyman title 'Macready of Tonypandy' – and later sent to command in Northern Ireland at the time of Carson's threatened 'loyalist' rebellion, the morning of the strike had found him, as Adjutant-General, making arrangements for army units to take over the policing of the capital.

But, by the afternoon of the following day this trouble-shooting son of the celebrated Victorian actor, Charles Macready, friend of Dickens, had been presented, to his disgust, with a startling change of role and a change of uniform as well.

At the insistence of the Prime Minister, he had been offered the post of Commissioner of the Metropolitan Police Force, in place of the unfortunate Sir Edward who had been obliged to resign. And despite the insistence of the Prime Minister, Sir Nevil had very promptly refused it.

Only when he realised that the King himself, profoundly shocked by the evidence of disaffection in the police force, was anxious for him to take the job did he reluctantly give way.

The Premier had sacrificed Sir Edward Henry, his scapegoat for the troubles of the past. He now had his 'strong man' for the troubles of the future.

On Wednesday, September 4th 1918, I installed myself at
Scotland Yard. The building with its long dark passages could
never exude cheerfulness, and at this particular time a settled
atmosphere of nervousness and gloom seemed to have invested
the place. Everybody was quite polite, but evidently not enthusiastic at the advent of a soldier who, from the newspaper
of a couple of weeks before, might justly be imagined to com-
bine the disrespect of constitutional methods of a Colonel
Pride with the flabby incapacity of a Bourbon . . .

Macready, as he eased himself unwillingly into Sir Edward's
empty chair, had recent memories of his own bitter quarrel with
the 'frocks': Whitehall's 'interference' in the running of his army
department having led to a furious reaction that had scandalised
the politicians and had been followed by outråged charges that
he had treated Parliament with contempt.

Now, looking at his new staff, he felt morale was at a danger-
ously low point and needed dramatic heightening. The thought
was a challenge, and his outlook brightened.

Discipline, he resolved, must be regained, but rank and file
grouses remedied. Confidence in the importance of their job
must be restored among the men by bringing in more praise and
fewer pinpricks. The Home Office and Treasury officials, whose
red tape had strangled his predecessor's attempts at reform, must
be taught to keep their distance. And, should the Union leaders
grow too bold with their success then he, Macready, must be
quick to slap them down.

It was a formidable task the Commissioner set himself. A man
less courageous – or less arrogant, said some – would have opted
for measures more limited and safe. But the 'Prussian' as the left-
wing *Herald* saw him, was not much given to thinking small, or
baulking at odds.

Self-willed, self-opinionated, yet remarkably clear-headed in
times of crisis, this dapper, immaculately-tailored character had
shown not only the Rhondda rioters but also the influential coal

owners, who had hitherto considered the army to be at their personal disposal, the force of his displeasure. Nor, when commanding in Northern Ireland, had he hesitated to risk unpopularity in the service by his lack of sympathy for the reactions of his brother officers, the Curragh 'mutineers'. Now that he had accepted the job he had not wanted, no-one must meddle in the way he chose to operate. His advent was greeted by the cosily entrenched bureaucrats at the Home Office with almost as much alarm as that created among the Labour radicals, to whom his name smacked of militarist reaction.

New brooms sweep clean and Sir Nevil, it was obvious from the record, was going to raise a hell of a lot of dust. There were fears over where that dust was going to settle.

However, for the first few days of his regime Macready was content to look and learn. Among his subjects of study was the history of the Union and that of the men behind it: the men who, without meaning to, had served to place him in command of this unexpected field. Nothing if not thorough in his methods, he was an enthusiast for the army dictum of 'First know your Enemy . . .'

It was in 1912 that first public mention was made of a Police Union, at that time confined in its recruiting to the London area. Brain child of ex-Inspector John Syme, whose extreme reaction to an act of injustice inflicted on him by his superiors had led to his dismissal from the service, it appeared in an advert in the *Police Review*.

To judge by the size and location of its headquarters – a newspaper shop in Chapter Street, Westminster – there was little cause to fear that the new organisation would bring about a revolution in the Yard. Nor, with the exception of Syme, whose spectacular efforts to draw attention to his case had repelled former sympathisers and earned him the reputation of a crank, were its sponsors in any way formidable. But even the mention of a 'union' of policemen was sufficient to agitate the dovecots of Whitehall.

At about the same time as Syme's announcement of this

organisation 'to safeguard the police against official tyranny and injustice', a police journal had suggested, very tentatively, the formation of a police federation 'on which the constables might confer and make joint representations to their superiors on any point at issue.'

To both of these proposals, though the latter was so seemingly modest in its ambition and tone, came an immediate counter-blast: a Police Order which, displayed in every station in the Metropolitan area, stated:

> It has come to the knowledge of the Commissioner that attempts have been made to induce members of the Metropolitan Police to join a federation or union. The Commissioner desires to point out that membership of such an association is prohibited by Standing Orders and that any man serving who violates those orders or incites others to violate them, renders himself liable to disciplinary proceedings, which can result in his dismissal from the force.

Henry, with memories of the odium incurred by the force during two previous small-scale attempts at strike action in 1872 and 1890, had made his meaning all too clear, and the *Review* dutifully decided to argue the federation cause no longer.

But the Commissioner's warning to the advocates of the Union had lesser luck. Inflamed by the attempt to stifle his brain-child while it was still in the cradle, Syme merely went underground; recruiting members but never publishing their names or numbers, and organising secret meetings which even the CID could rarely penetrate.

In 1914, what had become known as 'the right to confer' came briefly into the open again, with questions in Parliament, but those who argued that the police were grossly handicapped by being deprived of a right enjoyed by all other working citizens were partly silenced by the Home Secretary's promise that: 'The police who accept the position shall have as great benefits in pay and hours of labour, and in other conditions, as would be given to any other class of public servant who has a trade union behind him.'

Unfortunately, such fine words came to nothing. Or rather, only half-a-crownsworth more than nothing. In Syme's day the minimum rate for a Metropolitan PC was 27 shillings [£1.35] a week, and the maximum after twenty years' service was only ten shillings [50p] more. The Home Secretary had brought the minimum up to 30 shillings [£1.50], but because of the war the hours of labour worsened. Rest days were shelved for the duration.

In the first fine flush of patriotism that accompanied the war's outbreak this had not seemed to matter. Over four thousand members of the Metropolitan force went to the Front, and others volunteered for additional duties to fill the gap these had left behind them. They gave warnings of the approach of the dreaded Zeppelins, made sure that blackout regulations were observed, shepherded crowds seeking refuge in the tube stations, mounted guard on the docks and vital installations. And all these 'extras' they did without extra pay.

By 1915, however, this splendid response to the many demands that were made upon them had begun to flag. And the Union, though still banned, received a record intake of recruits. What had sparked off this reaction was basically the excessive rise in the cost of living. When it came to keeping a wife and children fed, patriotism most certainly was not enough!

Worse followed. In an effort to steady the costs spiral the Government clamped a wage freeze on the public sector, and the police – already at a disadvantage – were its principal victims.

As Douglas Massey, himself a former PC has recorded in his treatise *The Police Strike of 1919*: 'By late 1917 the wages of a policeman on top pay had increased from 40s. [£2.00] to 48s.0d. [£2.40] or a rise of 20 per cent. The wages of labourers in the engineering industry had risen from 22s.10d. [£1.14] to 48s.9d. [£2.44] an increase of 113 per cent, and the wages of skilled fitters had risen from 38s.11d. [£1.95] to 67s.4d. [£3.37] an increase of 75 per cent. The cost of living had been increased by 76 per cent.'

But grim though they were, these comparisons were made worse by the fact that although the police had lost their

17

weekly rest day and worked a seven-day week throughout the war, they received no overtime payment. Yet industrial workers were having no difficulty in doubling their wages with overtime.

By 1918, the average PC was receiving less than an unskilled labourer and only a third of the take home pay of a munitions worker.

'Profiteering', as one bitter policeman put it, 'is by no means confined to the so-called upper classes.'

Yet a policeman was supposed to keep up appearances, live in a 'respectable' dwelling – for which he got a so-called rent allowance of 2 shillings [10p] a week – and abstain from supplementing his earnings by taking a part-time job.

He was also expected to continue to accept a disciplinary code that had changed very little from that prevailing in the darkest days of the nineteenth century.

And if, forbidden to leave the force by wartime regulations, he was desperate enough to seek dismissal by committing misconduct, the punishment he incurred was a heavy fine, deducted from the pay packet whose very inadequacy had been the cause of his 'crime'.

Yet to all these manifest wrongs, authority turned a persistently deaf ear. Forbidden to demonstrate, forbidden to organise, the policeman presented no immediate problem to legislators and civil servants preoccupied in meeting the demands of those who could make their grievances felt by doing these things.

And by the time that Sir Edward Henry had concluded his calm and measured reappraisal of the pay scale of the men under his command, and the Treasury had begun its leisurely examination of the 'actuarial costing' of his scheme, there were PCs dropping of malnutrition in the street.

James Marston was not one of those who fell. As Chairman of the Union, he was fighting on his feet.

The exact opposite to the new arrival at the Yard, except in his unyielding obstinacy and almost Cromwellian conviction in the rightness of his cause, Marston was opposed to Macready's appointment from the start.

'God knows what the men saw in him,' the Commissioner

pondered, when retailing in his memoirs the story of their frequent clashes.

But despite this unflattering opinion of his capabilities Jim Marston was to achieve the rare distinction of ruffling his superior's carefully contrived composure; causing him on occasion to explode in exasperation and anger.

CHAPTER TWO

A Prussian at the Yard

'One man, when asked the cause of the strike, jerked his thumb towards the august buildings in Whitehall and said: "Dilly Dally. You'll find him in all these buildings."'

Recalling this incident, which occurred as he wandered through the crowd outside Number Ten, Basil Thomson was to add 'Unfortunately he was right. If at the outset of the agitation a scheme had been drawing up embodying the Government concessions and this had been communicated to the men, no strike would have taken place.'

And Sir Nevil Macready, not always of one mind with the head of the CID was to place similar blame for the crisis on the Home Office's 'tortoiseshell movements and antediluvian methods.'

'In view of the fact', he wrote, in his memoirs, *Annals of an Active Life* 'that the rates of pay were known to be in need of revision an immediate substantial temporary increase pending the elaboration of a permanent scheme would certainly have thinned the ranks of the union. It was a case where, in my opinion, the Commissioner would have been justified in metaphorically holding a pistol to the head or the tail of the Home Office.'

Unfortunately for Henry, his delay in doing so had turned the pistol against himself, and had guided his finger to the trigger.

Though subject to so much criticism for his handling of the events that led up to the Metropolitan police strike – he was too 'remote', too 'authoritarian', and too dedicated to doing things according to the 'Book' – Henry's downfall had been regarded with near consternation by those aware of his previous service to the State, service which more than merited his subsequent acceptance as 'one of the greatest policemen of our times'.

Henry had come to the Yard via the Indian Civil Service, the office of Inspector General of Police in Bengal, and a stint in South Africa where he had reorganised the civil police forces of Johannesburg and Pretoria shortly after the Boer surrender. An initiator, he had introduced the finger-printing system, against considerable opposition, a move subsequently copied by every other police force in the world. He had also greatly enhanced the status and effectiveness of photo identification – today's celebrated Rogues Gallery owes much to his efforts – and established a police training college.

But, strong though he was in energy and intellect, this precise and quietly-spoken official, dedicated to administration since his boyhood, was undoubtedly weak in the field of human relations.

Both in India and South Africa he had been accustomed to instant and unquestioning obedience. And, although personally an extremely kindly man, as was demonstrated in court when he pleaded for clemency to be shown to a would-be assassin who had pumped three bullets into him, was extremely conscious of 'the responsibility of rank' when in his official capacity. He was a father figure, who must know best . . .

To Sir Edward Henry the emergence of a Union to represent the men of his command had merely been the thin end of the wedge of 'bolshevism', and the 'right' to confer was an impertinent irrelevancy. If a man had a complaint then he should go through 'the proper channels', in other words lodge his complaint with his superior. And the implication of the fact that this superior might himself be the very subject of complaint still did not dim his belief that justice would be done. Critics said that he had modelled his regime on that of the British Raj, seldom showing himself in person to the 'natives', but delegating the day-to-day and tedious routine duties to his 'district' officers (the Superintendents) while he pursued his major, but leisurely, appraisal for the improvement of his empire.

Unfortunately for Sir Edward, just two years short of seventy, what may have been good for India in Victoria's Golden Jubilee year was not necessarily so for London, four decades later. And the District Administrators, however heavy the White Man's Burden, did not have to cope with the aspirations and grievances of such self-respecting characters as London policemen, endowed by the very nature of their job with a rich capacity for scepticism. Here were no great subscribers to the virtues of paternalism, however well-intended: and the Superintendents themselves were seldom father-figures.

'The Commissioner,' Macready recorded, 'was dependent for his information on the reports of his superintendents, men of unblemished character, who had been promoted mainly for length of service and good conduct, but who in many instances were not capable of commanding and handling divisions which in some cases numbered 1,500 men.'

Reports, he claimed, were often coloured in order to give the impression that all was well in certain divisions when they most certainly were not. And, appalled that his predecessor had been assured that there was no cause for uneasiness only two days before the outbreak of the Strike, he struck out at the proof this offered of 'want of touch' between the men and the higher officials.

Indeed, it was this want of touch, 'together with the injudicious handling of the men in certain divisions,' that had sparked off the 'insidious campaign' to form the Union. Things would have to be altered.

Nor was the new Commissioner even mildly amused to hear that, on the all-too-rare occasions when they visited the stations, the Superintendents had to rely on antiquated horse-drawn traps for their official conveyance.

This led to situations 'where the groom or someone else would pass the word by telephone and, of course, by the time the horse had been harnessed and had solemnly trotted over the intervening distance, everything was spick-and-span at the station on the great man's arrival.'

Regardless of the feelings of the finance departments, he promptly had the laggard 'Supers' equipped with motor cars.

Next item on Sir Nevil's list of changes was the role of the

Chief Constables. At the time of his appointment there were three people of this rank in the Metropolitan Police Force, but he considered that their functions were 'very nebulous'. They were usually to be found sitting in the Yard, their work confined to 'dabbling with important papers' he complained. They neither sat nor dabbled much longer.

Pursuing his quest for better communications between periphery and centre, he took advantage of the resignation of one of these high-ranking officials to promote – against all 'seniority' arguments – a bright young Superintendent in his stead, and imported, again defying much criticism, an army officer, an old friend, to increase the strength of the Chief Constables to four.

And then, this done, he sent all four of them packing, each to command one of the four districts into which – another Macready move – the Metropolitan Police Area had been split; the divisions in turn being grouped beneath them.

Each Chief Constable was to live within the borders of his district, maintain continual contact with the Superintendents, and be responsible for everything that happened in the divisions.

He was also given the task of advising the Commissioner 'on the merits and demerits of the higher ranks as they came forward for promotion.' Seniority was no longer to be made the main criterion for an officer's advancement.

Intensely energetic and, unlike his predecessor, possessing the great advantage of knowing that, owing to the peculiar circumstances of his appointment, the Whitehall establishment was scarcely likely to challenge the way he chose to utilise that energy, it was obvious from the start that the New Broom was indeed determined to sweep clean.

Equally obvious was the fact that, so far as the reform of the police hierarchy was concerned, he was succeeding in comparatively easy style. But the problems posed by this administrative operation were, as he fully recognised, comparatively minor in their size and implications to those that would confront him when he switched to his main target: the still triumphant but hostile and nervous Union.

*   *   *

23

'Another triumph for Lloyd George!' Applauding the ending of the Police Strike in its leader column of 2 September, the *Daily Mirror* quoted a policeman as saying: 'Mr Lloyd George has done straight off the reel what the others have been tinkering at for years.'

The paper had praised the Prime Minister for 'seeing at once that the greater part of the men's demands were fair and reasonable,' and had added that 'the police are to be congratulated on having accomplished a very just and equitable change in their wage system.'

But, this said, the *Mirror* had then gone on to emphasise: 'At the same time the Prime Minister is to be congratulated over his wise decision not to grant official recognition to a police union, although he has expressed the wish that some machinery should be put into operation under which members of the force can bring their grievances before the authorities.

'It should never be forgotten that the police are a semi-military body. They are an army defending law and order. They are the custodians of the peace.

'An officially recognised trade union of policemen,' said the *Mirror*, 'might well lead to an officially recognised trade union of soldiers and sailors.'

Unwittingly, the paper had summarised in those last two paragraphs the fear that was probably the driving force behind the former Adjutant-General's actions as Commissioner, and his attitude towards NUPPO, and to those who led it.

Authoritarian but possessed of a strong sense of justice – 'fair play' he would have called it in the public-school style of the day – Sir Nevil Macready was genuinely concerned at the disabilities incurred by the lower ranks and was ready and willing to better their lot, but the idea of a Police Union was anathema to one of his upbringing and outlook.

A Union would mean that the police in times of industrial conflict would be torn between the demands of the Government and those of organised labour. Worst of all, as the *Mirror* had remarked, it could lead to a demand for similar unions to represent the armed forces.

With the mutiny at Verdun a recent terrifying memory, and with a vivid perception of the part played by the Soldiers' and Sailors' Committees in the disintegration of Tsarist Russia accompanied by the full horrors of civil war, the very thought of anything so revolutionary as a serviceman's union was sufficient to induce paranoia in even the most liberally-minded British brasshat: and Sir Nevil, whatever his virtues, was very far from liberal.

His opponents were as yet unaware of the fact that he had visited the War Minister on the first morning of the recent Strike and, as Adjutant-General, had urged him to stiffen the Government against what he feared they might be tempted to do, namely capitulate to the Strike leaders' demand for a Union. But though relieved that this had not occurred, he had been disgusted by the way in which the issue had – as he foresaw – been postponed rather than quashed, and had expressed his forebodings about the future.

But however damning his criticisms of the ambivalence of the 'frocks' his mistrust of the Police Strike leaders – not the men – was even stronger.

A friend was once said to have quizzed him on how he would feel if a Police Union, in exchange for official recognition, abjured in its constitution the right to strike, and also renounced affiliation with other unions. What would he think of recognition in such a case? Would not that remove the objections advanced by Government?

Dryly, Sir Nevil is said to have answered that such a union was already in existence with the right to strike, or affiliate, abhorred even by its militant founder, and later barred explicitly by its rules. And that was no less a 'Union' than NUPPO, before its leaders rescinded the rules, and struck for recognition!

Apocryphal or not the comment, like so many others circulating in the tense and emotion-charged period when Commissioner and Union were getting each other's measure for the future, portrayed only one side of the picture, but to many it must have seemed rounded enough.

Back in 1913 even 'that madman' Syme had been opposed to

the idea of policemen taking strike action, while the moderates of the palace revolution that later ousted him from leadership had gone even further in their condemnation, barring members from striking by three clauses in the rule book. And yet, when Marston and Co. had come to power, the rules had gone out of the window.

'The Executive Committee of the National Union of Police and Prison Officers hereby gives notice to the Metropolitan Police Authorities that non compliance with the above demands by 12 midnight will necessitate the suspension of clauses A, B and C of the Union's Rule 2.'

Macready, who did his homework, could recite those words by heart. They came at the end of the Union's ultimatum of 27 August, and the start of the strike that overthrew his predecessor. Union rules lasted only for so long as the leaders thought fit: such was the moral that he drew from it all, and the fact that the 'mutiny' had been the work of men despairing at getting redress any other way, was regrettable but irrelevant to his dominant premise: a Union in the police force would be a bad thing for the army, a bad thing for the country, and a bad thing probably for the police themselves.

Sir Nevil, with the best of motives, was out to scotch the Union, come what may.

Agitators . . . demagogues . . . dangerous radicals . . . the men who had acquired these endearing descriptions in the orderly columns of *The Times* and the *Morning Post* were not of a type content merely to prepare for trouble. Sensitive to slight, and jealous of power, it is fair to say that they went out looking for it.

Deeply suspicious, and with very good reason, of the motives that inspired Macready's much publicised improvements of the lot of the rank and file, the NUPPO leaders had fired the first shots of what could have been a new rebellion within four days of the new Commissioner's arrival. But, excercising an uncharacteristic restraint, he had refused to fire back, and the affair had ended in an uneasy truce.

This initial skirmish had arisen from the Prime Minister's

ambiguity over the nature of 'the authorised organisation' that would represent the men, and in particular the role of the Union.

With nothing from the flustered Cabinet or Home Office to act as guide regarding these two crucial points of the settlement, and probably fearing that undue delay might result in a version from the Strike organisers that would make the Union position unassailable, Macready, with typical self-assertiveness, had decided to go it alone.

Authoritatively, he had laid down a scheme whereby each division would elect by secret ballot a delegate for what he called a Representative Board, 'to discuss all matters concerning the force, and bring them to my notice.'

And, this done, he had called a meeting of men, one from each of the twenty-six divisions, in order to explain the scheme, 'and incidentally to make their acquaintance too'.

Marston's furious reaction to this unilateral move, made without any reference to the Union Executive, Macready had subsequently greeted with bland, but quite unconvincing, surprise.

Yet the Commissioner had been circumspect enough not to push that early dispute to extremities, and the Norfolk man had reluctantly to relax his massive muscles.

Seemingly the soul of sweet reason, Macready had agreed to the Union Executive seeing the Home Secretary and presenting their amendments to the plan. He had also approved the approval of those amendments, and masking his feelings, the lifting of the ban on PCs joining the Union, 'this provided it did not interfere with the discipline of the force'. And he had even hidden his discomfiture when the Union leaders had the last laugh in the elections.

Despite the secret ballot on which he had lain such store, every one of the Executive had been elected to the Board. Carmichael's boast had been made good, or so it appeared. The Representative Board *was* the Union, under a different name!

All the same the NUPPO's leadership well knew their opponent was not one to relish reverses, particularly a reverse as shattering as this. His pride would be outraged: so too would be his principles. He was as obstinate as Jim Marston, and a lot more subtle. As events seemed to prove.

The section houses – homes to many of the PCs – had long been noted for their austere and cheerless style: Macready took special pains to brighten them up. Such luxuries as carpets took over from bare boards. Armchairs were provided instead of upright wooden chairs. Canteen facilities began to show considerable improvement.

Macready's concern for his 'troops' expressed itself in many different ways. The refreshment allowance – static for decades at one shilling [5p] a week – was doubled, despite the inevitable Treasury protests. He abolished the iniquitous system whereby a man who had committed some minor disciplinary offence was forced to mortgage part of his salary each week in paying off a fine. And, where Sir Edward had been a remote and lonely figure, seldom seen except by those on duty at Scotland Yard, Macready paid frequent and unheralded visits to the stations, always making a point of chatting with the men.

Soon – understandably – the word began to get around that the new Commissioner was a likeable and approachable sort of chap. Very much the boss, of course, but also a boss who cared. The only place where his behaviour did not go down well – equally understandably – was among the members of the Union Executive, who were irritated and dismayed.

Even though it was in full accord with the genuine and soldier-like sense of responsibility towards the lower ranks that Macready had shown throughout his army career, his attitude merely confirmed the Executive's worst suspicions. In his every move they could sense an attempt to undermine them and the Union.

Authority had yielded too gracefully to their demands to be genuine about it: or so they felt. Macready was trying to ensure that their gains were not maintained.

By Christmas the last vestige of goodwill engendered by the settlement had disappeared, except for Marston's faith – pathetically mistaken – in the Union having a powerful friend in the person of Lloyd George. The 'Prussian' on the other hand was definitely an enemy, and to be treated as such on every possible occasion.

Whenever Sir Nevil had need to meet the Representative
Board both Marston and Sergeant Thiel, whose reinstatement –
following dismissal for his Union activities – had been a keypoint
in the September settlement, made obvious their personal antipathy.

And Macready, in turn, seemed to enjoy – indeed provoke –
their blustering rudeness by his air of nonchalance and the
teasing repartee, of which he was a master. Needling them with
gentle ridicule, and deflating their pretensions, he brought out
the worst in them.

Faced by what he called 'misrepresentations' of the views he
expressed to Board members, he boldly served up a resumé of
each meeting, which was fixed to station notice-boards.

'He kept us well posted!' an old Union hand later stated. 'He
told us a damn sight more than our own lot ever did.'

Yet, had they but known it, the Commissioner's assumption of
superiority was more apparent than real as he examined the results of the first quarter of his tenure.

Before the Strike there had been less than a thousand members in the Union, of whom probably only a quarter were active.
By Christmas there were more than twenty times that figure,
and their numbers were growing daily. No longer confined to the
capital, the NUPPO tentacles had stretched out to most of the
major cities. Marston and Thiel had received rousing receptions
in the provinces, and provincial representatives now had a place
on the Executive.

In short, the success of the Strike and the lifting of the ban on
Union membership had transformed NUPPO from a well-
intentioned but ineffectual grouping of radicals and eccentrics
based in London, into a national movement, and worst of all –
from authority's point of view – other unions were beginning to
take notice. Still 'unrecognised' by Whitehall, the Police Union
was exchanging fraternal delegates with its big brothers in organised labour, including the ever-aggresive docks, transport
and miners' unions.

To Macready it must have seemed a frustratingly poor return

for all his efforts, and in some respects rather bewildering. However excessive the fury his name induced in Marston and the rest of the Executive diehards, there was no doubt at all that his popularity was high among the rank and file. Unfortunately, there were factors making for discord that were quite outside his control.

The increase in pay and allowances obtained in September had appeared substantial – bringing a Constable's maximum pay up to £3.00 a week plus 7/6d (37½p) War bonus – but already it was being eroded by inflation. Soon, unless something additional was arranged, the men would be almost as badly off as they were before the settlement. True, a committee headed by Lord Desborough, had been established to enquire into the whole field of police pay and conditions. But neither Macready nor the rank and file expected very speedy results. Governments introduced committees when they wished to buy time.

Another major hindrance to the Commissioner's policy of placating and improving the lot of the bulk of the force, thus making NUPPO redundant, was the confusion that had arisen from Lloyd George's comments about refusing the Union recognition in wartime.

Had he realised that, within eight weeks of his speaking, the war that had then seemed to be going on for ever, would have been halted by the Armistice, doubtless the PM would have chosen his words with more circumspection.

As it was, they were now played back, to provide ammunition for the militants, drumming into the uncommitted and the weak, that recognition was just around the corner, and the Union would be master of the morrow.

In such circumstances it was not surprising that reports of indiscipline among the rank and file were on the increase, nor that the Executive's attitude was becoming ever more arrogant. As incident followed incident, those close to the Commissioner pondered on how long he could keep his calm, and privately forecast a typhoon when once it broke. They were not to be disappointed.

The crunch came on 19 February over yet another of the several 'differences of interpretation' that were blossoming between the Board and the Commissioner.

Disagreeing with the content of one of his orders, the delegates forwarded a protest to the Home Secretary and passed a resolution that opened, 'In view of the fact that the Commissioner may endeavour wilfully to delay the reply of the Home Secretary . . .'

The 'typhoon' immediately followed.

Furious with anger, Macready stormed along to the Commissioner's Library, which he had lent to the Board for its deliberations, only to have the door slammed in his face, and the key turned in the lock.

For a few breathless seconds stunned police messengers were entertained to the near-incredible sight of their usually poised and impeccably-mannered chief battering with his fists on the door panels before one of the Board delegates, having second thoughts, admitted him.

Macready's counter-blast to 'being called a liar', as he saw it, was to accuse those who had framed the resolution of gross indiscipline. And he concluded his outburst with the threat that never again would he receive a deputation from a Board that had so outrageously abused its role. To the delegates' consternation he was to prove that he meant what he said.

Unknown to its members, the Board's days were already numbered. And the incident had served merely to confirm Sir Nevil in a decision taken a good month before. On 17 January he had written to the new Home Secretary, Edward Shortt:

That the system of having a representative board is sound in a large force like the Metropolitan Police I am convinced, because under the present organisation it would be impossible otherwise to get at the pulse of the men. At the same time, the present Board came into being just after the strike, and many men with strong union leanings were elected. Indeed, not long ago the members of the executive committee were made ex-officio members of the union executive with, no doubt, the

31

idea that the Representative Board would really be a union executive under another name.

In thus expressing his dissatisfaction at the way in which the Board, his brain-child, had been taken over by the very radicals it had been designed to thwart, Macready was complaining about an embarrassment for which he himself was largely to blame.

He had established the Board on a one-tier basis, with Inspectors, Sergeants and Constables lumped together for the election of representatives. Yet surprisingly for one so seldom accused of deficiency in foresight, he had been taken completely off balance by the predictable result.

With twenty-six Constables elected, as against only five Sergeants and one solitary Inspector, not only did the interests of the PC's take priority but, being mostly nominated by NUPPO, they had been able to turn the Board into a rostrum for the Union.

'It has many times been brought to my notice that the result of having sergeants mixed up with the men is prejudicial to discipline,' Macready ruefully recorded.

The time had come to part them, and brave the Union's wrath in doing so.

On 4 March, only thirteen days after the clash in the Commissioner's Library, members of the Board received notification from their adversary that the organisation was to be scrapped, and four separate groupings established in its place.

Constables, Sergeants, Inspectors and Superintendents, as from 1 April each rank would vote solely for representatives of that rank, to serve on a board representing that rank's interests alone.

And, just to rub the lesson thoroughly home, the shocked delegates were also told:

In the opinion of the Commissioner judging from his experience during the last six months, it is impossible that the discipline necessary to the efficiency of the force can be maintained if the interests of officers are placed in the hands of lower ranks, or if, in discussions which affect the force as a whole, officers sink their rank and place themselves on the same level as those who are under their orders on actual duty. A matter like this can not be treated in the same way as if officers and men were engaged in sport . . .

Even for Marston, not normally given to historical analogy, here was a clear case of 'Divide and Rule' and, once the Executive had recovered, their protest was loud and clear. 'The constitution of the Board had been violated,' they said. The Home Secretary must grant them an interview. That interview, held three days later, was to have – unfortunately for the Union men – a most disastrous sequel.

CHAPTER THREE

Prelude to Battle

'The Home Secretary is more than sympathetic, and has urged that the force should be paid in accordance with its duties and responsibilities. . . .' This description of the new Home Office attitude to the pay issue was given by Sir Nevil Macready, in an address to the men designed to counter NUPPO charges that 'reactionary militarists' were aiming to sell them short. In part at least his summary was accurate.

Shortt shared the Commissioner's irritation over the way in which governmental parsimony and a complacent bureaucracy had served to bring about the Strike and the current disaffection. He was as determined as Macready himself to get a new deal underway that would be generous enough to pacify the force and enable it to settle down. What Sir Nevil did not mention, however, was the strength of this distinguished lawyer's antipathy to the trade union movement in general, and his determination to eliminate 'outside influences' from the police.

In Edward Shortt, the Commissioner had found a man after his own heart: a man who would give full support to his authority in the event of the showdown that he was now convinced was inevitable. Shortt's principles were as rock-firm as his solid jawline, jutting like the bows of a dreadnought from beneath the close-shaved cheeks and the broad protruding brow that had made him the delight of the political cartoonists and the terror of hostile witnesses. What he lacked in charisma, he made up in character, a quality in which Sir Nevil had hitherto found Whitehall to be somewhat deficient.

Worded in characteristically tactless style, Marston's demand for an interview had been received with no enthusiasm at the

Home Office, but from the moment that Shortt agreed to meet him, together with a delegation of other 'representatives of the Board,' it was obvious that the Union leader and his colleagues had been caught on the hop.

With no alternative plan of their own that could measure up to that put forward by the 'violator' Macready, they were left to argue solely the maintenance of the *status quo* and realising that on that point too their efforts were getting them nowhere against Shortt's adamant insistence that the existing system must go, tempers, already frayed, completely snapped.

They would not support the new scheme, Marston announced. They would recommend that the men refuse to co-operate. And they would urge a boycott of the elections for places on the new 'bosses' boards'.

It was a brave declaration, expressive of the frustration of men who, only a few weeks back, had felt themselves to be on the commanding heights – arbiters of their destiny, and that of their comrades too. It was also a very unwise one. Within days Shortt had given his approval to Macready's counter-attack, delivered in the form of a Police Order.

In view of the interference of the National Union of Police and Prison Officers with the discipline of the Service, and the inducement to members of the force to withhold their services, the Commissioner with the approval of the Secretary of State calls upon all members of the force to forthwith sever their connection with such union. The Commissioner would point out that any member of the force failing to comply with this direction will be liable to dismissal from the force.

Posted on all station notice boards throughout the Metropolitan Police area, the order mentioned the fact that Shortt had appointed a Committee to consider and report on the rates of pay, pensions and allowances of the police force throughout the country and stated that 'no legitimate grievance or well-founded complaint remains, or will be allowed to remain, uninvestigated.' But it added:

The Union of Police and Prison Officers does not act with the authorities as was hoped. On the contrary, certain members of the union have set the authority of the Commissioner at defiance. Its actions make the proper maintenance of discipline in the force impossible.

The Secretary of State, therefore, while giving the force assurances of sympathetic consideration in all matters touching its welfare, and while desiring to provide the force with all proper safeguards, has decided in the public interest that no member of the force, present or future, shall continue to be a member of or join the Union of Police and Prison Officers or any like association.

The challenge had been delivered. Marston was not the type to refuse to pick it up. And by now he had been joined by J. L. Hayes.

Judged by the sluggish rate of promotion then prevailing, Jack Hayes had risen to Sergeant's rank with meteoric speed. He had been only four years in the force at the time of his promotion, and had served only one of them on the beat. The rest had been office work, ably performed.

He was to rise in the Union with equally dazzling speed. Almost unknown at the time of the first Strike, this Johnny-come-lately was nominated by Marston as General Secretary on 25 March, only four and a half months before the second Strike.

The job was a full-time one, at £500 a year; by no means a paltry figure in relation to the standards of the day, and ironically Macready was sorry to see him take it.

Recounting in his memoirs how he endeavoured to dissuade this 'level-headed' officer from taking the Union post, the Commissioner added: 'However he would not be convinced, and said that in any case his new position would give him many opportunities in public life. When I pointed out of the window towards the Houses of Parliament and suggested that he might have ambitions in the direction of the "talking house" he half-jokingly admitted the soft impeachment.'

From then on 'this good officer on whom I had my eye for future advancement' was to confirm that his superior had a good eye for form.

Of all the Union activists, Hayes – son of a police Inspector – was to prove the most talented and troublesome. He was a practitioner of subtleties, not one to rush in bull-headed. Why rush a barricade when you might perhaps outflank it?

Marston's taste for the more exotic terminology of revolution had served often to repel those who mistook the words for will. Hayes, except when deeming such phraseology expedient, was lucid, down to earth, and played up the everyday issues.

He was solidly respectable in appearance and firmly authoritative in manner, attributes that were useful assets when dealing with men who, in the main, were new recruits to militancy.

One-occasion-only rebels as they were, these men could easily be embarrassed by the unfamiliarity of their role and feel that, ideologically, they were very far from home. To part them, however briefly, from the habits of a lifetime the cause had to seem impeccable, the alternative non-existent. Hayes did his best to persuade them on both counts.

As Leonard Petchey, at that time a PC in the Liverpool Police, remembers him: 'Hayes was always well turned-out, but never flash. He had shoulders broad enough for the weak to cry on. His moustache was neat and well-trimmed, in sharp contrast to Jim Marston's. Appropriately, Marston's was thick and fierce and shaggy.'

And to Richard O'Keeffe, also of the Liverpool force, 'Jack Hayes was a clever fellow. No doubt about that. Even though we were on opposite sides throughout the crisis I always admired the way he could push his views forward and, above all, the way he could keep his calm.'

Even after Macready's blow to the Union's solar plexus, Hayes showed no signs of indulging in the current punch-drunk frenzy.

While Marston had played into the Commissioner's hands by defiantly telling Shortt that he should be received as Chairman of the Union and not merely as a member of the Representative

Board, Hayes in a subsequent statement had neatly side-stepped the recognition hurdle.

Reflecting that this had been 'promised by the Prime Minister', who was therefore morally bound to bring it about, he contented himself by saying that recognition would follow the day when the War Cabinet gave place to a peacetime successor.

In fact, in the present instance, the issue was not important; he insisted that the real and vital point of grievance was the Commissioner's violation of the Representative Board.

This foretaste of the technique that the former Sergeant was to deploy in the interests of NUPPO served not only to irritate his former chief but also to win the sympathy of moderates, both inside and outside the force. They were far more impressed by Hayes's 'hurt-rather-than-annoyed' reproaches to Macready than by Marston's threats of 'extreme action' to come. They joined their voices to those of the Commissioner's more partisan attackers. His action had been 'arbitrary' they claimed; and deliberately provocative. Needless to say, the *Daily Herald* made a regular meal of it.

Another sign of the new and effective style emerging in the Union leadership came when Hayes was called upon to testify to the Desborough Committee, which was at last commencing its review of the pay and pensions problems of the police forces as a whole.

To the surprise and probable disappointment of Macready, accustomed to the way in which Marston was prone to spoil even the best of arguments by too much heat and self-righteous indignation, Hayes made no reference to NUPPO and its alleged persecution but concentrated solely on the questions put to him, winning much goodwill in the process by the cogency of his address and – deceptively – moderate manner.

However, when he later attempted to open up a direct correspondence with the Commissioner on the subject of the Representative Boards, this twenty-seven-year-old aspiring politician found himself confronted by a less receptive audience.

Noting that Hayes was acting in his capacity as General Secretary of the Union, Sir Nevil, scenting a trap, bleakly answered:

'I can take no cognisance of an organisation which has no official connection with the Metropolitan Police.'

But the boldest, some said the cheekiest, stroke played by Jack Hayes was when he formally applied to the Commissioner, in conformity with the Trafalgar Square Act of 1844, for permission for the Union to hold a meeting there.

This was for the purpose of demanding the reinstatement of a union official, Constable Spackman, sacked after defiantly writing 'No Action' across Macready's order regarding the new Board elections. It was also to demand Macready's instant departure.

'I was a good deal amused,' the latter wrote in later years, 'at the Union having to make application to me for permission to hold a meeting of which one of the principal objects was to kick me out of the Yard. Some of my more serious-minded assistants were I think deeply shocked, and were against my giving permission.'

Weighed against this, however, was the thought that such a refusal 'would only be playing the Union game, and also it is not everybody who can claim to be the hero of a Trafalgar Square meeting!'

So the demonstration went ahead, and Sir Nevil, with amiable effrontery, robbed the affair of much of its drama by going along to watch it.

By then it was becoming increasingly obvious that such incidents were not ends in themselves, but part of a broader purpose; one plain enough to the main protagonists, though not as yet to the general public.

A battle in classic style is preceded by much skirmishing, and Macready was too old a soldier not to know a skirmish when he saw one. He was also too much of a general not to welcome what it heralded; his final decisive struggle with the Union.

A new Police Bill based on the Desborough Report was being prepared for Parliament; it would give members of the force a chance of expressing their views through a Police Federation modelled largely on Macready's representative board. But it would also make it illegal for a police officer to belong to a trade union as such. Unless they decided to abdicate, or Marston's 'friend', Lloyd George, put a stop to it, the Union leaders must fight or go under.

There had been talk of a second strike as far back as November, when Sir Nevil had felt the attitude of the NUPPO officials to be so 'overbearing' that, fearing as he put it a *coup d'état*, he had secretly taken steps to bring detachments of soldiers into ninety key stations, 'in order to give protection and confidence to the men who might remain loyal.'

Since then, the Union had come to boast a membership of over 40,000 and it was obvious that, should there be a strike, its effects would no longer be confined to the Metropolitan area.

The Head Constables of such important forces as those of Manchester and Swansea had reported worrying symptoms of militancy in the ranks, for which they put the blame largely on NUPPO 'agitators' from London.

Yet there were those who felt, and Macready was among them, that the Union's growth of influence was more apparent than real.

It was natural enough that, following its September success, and the subsequent improvement in pay and conditions, the Union should find the enrolment of recruits a comparatively simple matter, particularly since the Government's agreement to lift the ban on membership. But would this mean that a national strike call would meet with a truly national response? Not only Macready, but Shortt as well, was ready to stake his all in doubting it.

For, paradoxically, those very improvements with which the Union had been credited had created in turn grave problems for its leadership. Together with Macready's reformist moves, they had served to allay much of the frustration and sense of injury that had driven the non-political mass of the Metropolitan force to follow (what was then) the small but radical minority who had so boldly launched rebellion.

And now that the Desborough Committee, spurred on by the Commissioner's persistent prodding, had actually got down to doing business, there were hopes of further, even larger, improvements to dampen rank-and-file zeal for Marston's revolutionary solutions.

Furthermore, it had become apparent to Macready that a fratricidal battle for power was being waged inside the Union's top Executive Committee. Although unpublicised, casualties had been heavy.

First to fall had been PC Ernest Harrison, who had played a key part in both the overthrow of the erratic John Syme and the successful planning of the September strike. Harrison had been accused by Marston of being 'a spy for Macready', and promptly sacked.

Next had come the turn of another Union veteran, its acting secretary, John Crisp, who resigned after yet another row involving the fiery Chairman.

Crisp's defection had followed a Committee move to make Marston General Secretary – the £500-a-year job later given to Hayes – and pay Thiel £312 a year as full-time organiser in the provinces.

A storm of protest from the branches, claiming that the Committee should have held a ballot of the membership, greeted this 'unconstitutional' proposal, and even when the leaders summoned a mass rally of members in the Albert Hall, the result was to provide the Commissioner with further cause for cheer.

Thanks to the efficiency of his intelligence service, he was able to send the Prime Minister a full and detailed account of what had transpired at this 'private' function, described by one of the Hall's caretakers as the stormiest he had ever seen.

'Police Constable Marston, the president of the Union, was severely heckled, especially by representatives from the North of England, who wanted to know on what authority he and other officials had been appointed,' Sir Nevil wrote. 'His answers were apparently not satisfactory, and it came out that Marston's methods were too autocratic, and that he had summarily dismissed various union officials for defying his mandates.'

And then, as the Police Bill continued to move forward, and both adversaries narrowed still further the safety margin of their

collision course, the Commissioner could savour even more welcome tidings: the formidable Jack Hayes had over-reached himself.

Hayes had recognised as clearly as Macready the limitations of
the Union's apparently extensive membership. Nor did he share
Marston's excessive confidence in the goodwill of Lloyd George.

Contrary to all expectations, the Desborough Committee was
working really fast, and he shrewdly suspected that its recommendations would be generous.

Lloyd George had other problems than the Union's on his
hands, and must choose between conflicting and variously
weighted pressure.

But throughout these critical months of move and counter-
move Jack Hayes had before his eyes one dazzling prospect: that
of harnessing to the NUPPO wagon the massive strength of the
major unions.

As deeply convinced as his near-Marxist colleague of the ab-
solute necessity of a police union, he had many reservations on
the wisdom of trying to 'go it alone'. From the start, he had
wooed the ranks of organised labour for support, and so far his
efforts had met with reasonable success.

Not only was Carmichael said to have 'sewn up' the London
Trades Council, the Triple Alliance was also pledging aid. And
recently, thanks to some Freudian slip on the part of a senior
civil servant in the Ministry of Labour, the 'unrecognised'
National Union of Police and Prison Officers had been invited to
take part in the National Industrial Conference, sponsored by
the very same Government that was seeking to make the Union
unlawful!

Furious though they were at this ludicrous mistake neither
Shortt nor Macready could do anything to get the invitation –
once publicised – withdrawn.

Instead, as if this humiliation was not enough, they had then
been treated to the spectacle of the more radical elements at the
conference appointing Marston to serve on the Joint Committee
of Unions and Management. Hayes must have found it difficult

not to burst out laughing.

Indeed, by mid-May, it appeared that the objective for which this single-minded and determined man of method had striven so patiently, the support of organised labour should a police strike materialise, was almost within his grasp.

To persuade the trade union movement – and also the Home Office – that the mass of the NUPPO membership, despite all reports to the contrary, was firmly behind the leadership, the executive had meanwhile organised a strike ballot.

Instead of asking members if they would strike for recognition of the Union alone, a question which might have received a most embarrassing answer, the ballot's terms of reference – later denounced as 'contrived' – were for recognition, the reinstatement of Constable Spackman AND AN IMMEDIATE AND SUBSTANTIAL INCREASE OF PAY.

This pay issue was still unresolved and it was the major pre-occupation of the serving policeman. Hayes was therefore confident of receiving a massive 'Yes' in the ballot.

And he was equally confident that, once confronted by the implementation of this 'democratic mandate', Labour would not leave the police brothers to fight the battle on their own.

Accordingly, hoping to clinch the deal, he announced that a monster rally of NUPPO members, together with delegates and supporters from other unions, would be held in Hyde Park on 2 June. The results of the ballot would then be given to the crowd, and a historic blow delivered in the fight against the Police Bill.

Alas for such expectations. On 27 May, just six days short of the rally, an incident arose that threatened the whole Grand Design with disaster: a bloody clash between unruly members of the Left-wing Discharged Soldiers and Sailors Federation, seeking to march on Parliament, and men of the Metropolitan Police Force, sent to restrain them.

In a battle that raged along the entire length of Victoria Street, where road repairs were in progress, the mob used scaffolding poles and paving stones to inflict more than 150 casualties – over twenty of them serious – upon the police. And the police, in their turn, drew batons and, in a series of charges, gave back as good as they had received, or even better.

By the time it was all over the new-found accord between 'Met' and Left appeared to have vanished for ever, and the air was thick with Labour reproaches of police brutality.

To Hayes, this was a near-fatal setback. Speakers from the Federation had been invited to the rally, but how many of them would feel like responding after so bitter a prelude? Even the ever-faithful *Daily Herald*, while hinting darkly that Macready had provoked the trouble, criticised the PCs severely for their response. What price 'solidarity' now?

Placed in the horrific position of either supporting his members, and offending the leaders of organised labour, or of stating that the police had behaved badly, and thus bringing further dissent into the Union, Hayes must have reflected that this, of all occasions, required a cool head and silver tongue. For once, however, he was completely deficient in both.

In his desperate anxiety to placate the trade union movement, he issued a press statement on behalf of NUPPO that not only carried a fulsome apology to the demonstrators but also stated that 'the responsibility for the whole occurrence rests solely upon the Home Secretary and the Commissioner of Police.'

Worse, the statement went on to add that: 'We state emphatically that the only solution for occurrences of this kind is the democratisation of the police force, the ending of militarism in the Metropolitan Force, the full and complete recognition of the Union, and the closer linking up of the police with organised labour.'

And then, as if this was not enough in itself to placate his hoped-for allies, the 'level-headed' Hayes concluded: 'We appeal to the discharged soldiers and sailors not to judge the union on yesterday's happenings. Let them blame the Government, the Home Secretary, the Commissioner of Police, and the military system against which we are strenuously fighting. As a union we look upon our comrades in the workshops and from the Army as comrades.'

To many a NUPPO stalwart, still nursing the wounds inflicted by these 'comrades', this probably was the most humiliating cut of all.

Hayes had blundered, and blundered badly. Bent on appeasing the one side, he had alienated the other. And, while the men of the Metropolitan Police were the first to make him realise that fact, many in the provincial forces served to rub it home.

Within hours of his words appearing in the press — 'At first I couldn't believe it was Jack,' says Leonard Petchey — a tidal wave of resentment had risen in the branches, to break around the executive and leave it in disarray. And, from this upheaval, Macready was quick to gain advantage.

Just two days after Hayes's unexpected lapse, the Commissioner visited the Prime Minister, to present a request that previously had been refused him. And this time he came away with what he had sought: permission to publish an order that would not only inform all ranks that he was aware of plans for strike action but would also lay down what the penalty for that action would be.

In the previous crisis the police authorities had been unprepared, and had left the lower ranks without any clear-cut guidance as to what to do when confronted by militant pickets. Macready was determined that this error would not be repeated. More, though he did not labour the point to Mr Lloyd George at the time, the order would be so precise that it would serve to stop the Government from subsequently weakening and, under pressure, again making terms with the strikers.

'The order,' Sir Nevil was to recall in his memoirs, 'put the issue clearly before the force, and by indicating clearly that the Government would not be satisfied with half measures, acted as a counterblast to the insidious propaganda of the union that Labour was stronger than Government.'

Published on 30 May 1919, it stated:

It having come to the knowledge of the Commissioner that a movement is on foot to induce the Metropolitan Police to again withdraw from their duty to the State, although the Commissioner is confident that the great majority of the force have no intention of so doing, he considers that, in view of the events of August, 1918, it is necessary for him to make known clearly the consequences that will overtake any officer or man who may be led away by persons who place individual interests before those of the State.

It is to be distinctly understood by all ranks that any officer or man, of whatever rank, who fails to report in the ordinary course of duty, or when called upon, will be forthwith dismissed from the force. Such officer or man will under no circumstances be permitted to rejoin the Metropolitan Police, and dismissal will result in the loss of all service counting towards pension. The Commissioner will be unable to accept excuses that men are unable to parade or carry on their work owing to intimidation.

Officers and men will, if necessary, defend themselves by all legitimate means if interfered with in the execution of their duty.

Simultaneously, the Commissioner informed the Chief Constables and Superintendents under his command that in the event of a strike materialising:

Lists of officers or men who have failed to parade for duty will be rendered to the Commissioner daily, and the Commissioner holds the superintendents personally responsible that each case has been investigated, and that there is no doubt whatever that the officer or man has knowingly and wilfully withdrawn his services. The Commissioner will be at the Commissioner's office. Constant reports will be sent by telephone, telegraph or orderly.

His plans complete, Macready decided to sit back, and wait and see. The third of June, the date of the Rally, had already been widely tipped as the date of the National Strike call: but that was before the publication of his order. Would the rally with the consequences before it, still be called upon for action on the third, or would its outcome merely be a fresh flow of rhetoric? Only the event could show.

At the same time, to still further cool the temperature of the Union, Shortt let it be known that the Desborough pay awards would be substantial, and back-dated. Furthermore – and this was a master-stroke – there would be a generous cash payment on account.

The third of June came, and ended on a strong note of anti-climax. By the morning of the Rally the Commissioner's order had reached every member of the Metropolitan Force, and several of the provincial chiefs had issued similar warnings to their forces as well.

Men from the Yard, reporting back to Macready, stressed that though the crowd was a large one, its police content was far lower than had been expected. Sympathisers from other unions and 'trouble-seekers' in general made up the bulk of the on-lookers. These were waiting for the Executive to do what it was rumoured they would do, namely declare a strike. They were destined to wait in vain.

It did not take long for Macready's observers to realise that, whatever issues were to be decided at the rally, an immediate national strike was not among them.

Announcing the results of the controversial ballot, Hayes told the crowd that this had produced 44,539 votes in favour of strike action, with only 4,324 against. But then, having hailed this as a major union victory, he had begun to argue strongly against promptly following it up.

Macready, he said, was only too eager for trouble. 'Machine guns and tanks' had been moved into London to crush it. 'But we shall strike when it suits us,' he declared. 'General Macready will be disappointed.'

The Union would strike 'when they have removed the tanks', meanwhile the Executive would 'get at the Wizard of Wales'.

To the disgust of the few, the relief of the many, and the dis-comfiture of the crystal-gazers on both sides, 3 June had failed to produce the expected crisis.

CHAPTER FOUR

Hangman's Drop

The first time the PM realised that the 1918 Strike was happening, so they said, was when the PCs on duty at Number Ten withdrew their services, and a detachment of Guards infantry, arrived instead.

As both the Home Secretary and the then Commissioner of Police had specifically, and repeatedly, denied there was any unrest in the Metropolitan Police, and had then promptly departed from the scene for the autumn holiday, Mr Lloyd George's ignorance had been perfectly understandable.

The sequel had, of course, been unfortunate for these two distinguished public servants, 'caught bending' as malicious critics put it, but nobody was likely to catch Lieutenant General Sir Nevil Macready in such a posture of unpreparedness.

'If he bent at all,' a subordinate was later to comment, 'it was merely to put his ear close to the ground.'

Sir Nevil was indeed very much in touch with events, and as befitted the son of so celebrated a father, was also brilliantly adept in taking his cue from them.

It had been a fine touch of theatre that had induced him, on the eve of the Trafalgar Square rally called to demand his resignation, to leave the Yard, dine at his club, and in immaculate morning coat, with flower in buttonhole, turn up beside Nelson's column to observe the marching demonstrators and listen genially to the speakers, putting them quite out of countenance.

Nor had the family flair for captivating an audience deserted him when, within a fortnight of publishing that controversial Police Order of 30 May, he had departed completely from protocol, called on his own initiative a mass meeting of Constables,

and so won them over by his brisk address that the proceedings
had ended with the men giving him a standing ovation, and a
resounding rendering of 'He's a jolly good fellow'.

For a man condemned by the union as a 'Prussianised militarist' Sir Nevil had an astonishingly populist appeal: an advantage that he subsequently exploited to the full when he attacked
NUPPO's leadership for what he called 'a betrayal of trust, and
glorification of a thief'.

This had resulted from the disclosure by the *Police and Prison
Officers Journal* of the contents of a confidential memo outlining
contingency plans for military intervention in the event of a
police strike: a 'scoop' obtained when, as the Editor coyly explained, 'one of our comrades, somewhere in England, acted as a
naughty boy and stole a certain letter which a certain Chief Constable had written to the Secretary of State . . .'

Macready's subsequent intervention, and the injured tone he
adopted on that occasion, had made many a Union member feel a
bit of a cad.

But, just as Hayes could dissemble for the sake of the 'Cause'
and, when seeking to influence the Desborough Committee,
switch from the role of Tower Hill rabble rouser to that of busi-
nesslike moderate, and just as Marston, fulminating on the 'constitutional rights' of free Englishmen when addressing a police
audience, could glorify the Russian Revolution when among his
ideological kindred, so could Macready be accused of wearing
two faces in order to achieve his ends.

In fact, despite his self-righteous condemnation of the Union's
use of 'spies', Sir Nevil was not above resorting to a little espionage on his own account, and in general that espionage was remarkably effective.

At almost every union meeting his plain-clothes police were
present, to observe and report back. Their subsequent comments
were then sent direct to the Commissioner. He read them all.

In addition, Macready obtained copies of the Yard's intelligence summaries, prepared by agents posing as strong Union
supporters. Close links were also effected with Military Intelligence.

At that time much concerned with the subject of 'subversion', created, it was believed, by 'foreign interests', MI was including in its surveillance areas that would normally have been considered to be of purely civilian interest, a development that the former Adjutant-General had been quick to welcome.

A similar close liaison was maintained with the Home Office, with Shortt arranging that, although Macready's authority did not extend to police forces other than the Metropolitan, copies of correspondence relating to the Union's activities as a whole were made available to him, together with the department's minuted views and agreed replies.

Among the massive intake of suggestions the latter had received from those seeking to make their views felt on the police dispute and the possibilities of a settlement, was one that must have been received by the Commissioner with more than routine interest. Dated 4 June it appeared indicative both of a softening of acerbity in one of the leading provincial forces and – from the tone of the marginal comments of the Home Office – a toughening up of attitude in Whitehall.

Reporting on an amicable meeting between civic dignitaries and the police, Mr Charles Dobson, President of the Sheffield Trades Council had written to George Roberts, the area's MP: 'If there obtained the same confidence and good feeling throughout the service as was evident in the meeting . . . the trouble would be at an end. The local secretary [of NUPPO] made the following remark from the platform amid applause. "Our Chief, Major J. Hall-Dalwood is the finest man God ever made. The fact is the men love him."'

Moved by this remarkable example of accord, Mr Dobson had then gone on to suggest that a 'peace delegation', composed of local councillors and representatives of the local branch of the Police Union, should negotiate direct with the Home Office for an acceptable agreement.

Alas for such good intentions. 'The President of a local trades council is not an appropriate intermediary between a Borough Police Force and the Secretary of State,' Shortt had coldly appended to the file. After which a senior civil servant had advised: 'Say that the best means of securing a body to represent the members of all the different police forces is a subject which is receiving the Secretary of State's most careful consideration. He has noted Mr Dobson's letter, but is unable to receive the suggested deputation . . .'

Authority's stance was obviously stiffening.

But in vastly different mood to that of placatory Sheffield was a communication beneath the letterhead of the Liverpool-based Federation of Engineering and Shipbuilding Trade Unions.

At a representative meeting of the members of this Federation, held last evening, I was directed to write to you, taking the strongest possible exception to the attitude of the Home Office and the Government in declining to recognise the Police Union.

There is a strong feeling that this autocratic attitude is entirely out of touch with the times and, furthermore, is calculated to create friction with all sections of organised labour.

I am to point out that our members are prepared to support the police in any action they may take to obtain recognition.

You are especially urged to make representation to the Government with a view to recognising this as a legitimate and bona fides trade union.

The author was the future Sir Walter Citrine, labelled by a police report as 'dangerous'!

But Macready did not rely on confidential sources alone for indications of the Union's likely moves and potential backers. He also believed in studying his opponent's published attitudes and in doing so, absorbed, without any noticeable increase in his blood pressure or tendency to rush into libel litigation, the most outrageous attacks upon his character and motives.

Predictably, many of these came from the *Daily Herald* – 'the press trumpet of the Union', as he put it – but often the *Morning Post* was numbered among the Commissioner's critics, though for reasons very different from those of its Labour rival. In the view of the ultra-rightist *Post*, Macready was an appeaser!

The response of the man exposed to these two extremes of opinion was to order both newspapers and read them before breakfast. When the former launched its 'Macready Must Go' campaign, he had two of its posters pinned to the wall above his chair at Scotland Yard: this to embarrass Union callers.

Sir Nevil was also a keen student of the *Police and Prison Officers Journal*, and the assessments made by his agents of various trends therein.

'Nothing very striking here', was the comment attached to one issue of the magazine. 'The marked passage makes it pretty clear that the men's confidence shown in the past few weeks is due to some assurance of support by the Locomotive Engineers Union.'

It is unlikely that the Commissioner was unduly concerned by this discovery, namely that yet another powerful union had given NUPPO its 'assurance of support'. Both in the Ulster affair and the Tonypandy riots he had found that such assurances were not always followed up by vigorous action.

Again, he was fortified throughout his campaign by a firm belief – not universally shared – that the vast majority of the Metropolitan Police would resist a call for strike action now that their grievances over pay and conditions had been settled, and the issue was solely that of recognition of the Union.

As he was to record in his memoirs:

From the moment when the Bill had passed the Committee stage I knew that any moment the hotheads of the Union might make a last desperate throw for victory by calling a strike on the off-chance that the Government would be frightened into coming to terms with them.

The spirit of the force was, however, very different from what it had been several months before, and I felt convinced that not more than 3,000 men at an outside estimate would obey the call of the union, and was prepared to carry on even if the figure reached 5,000 without invoking outside assistance in the shape of the military.

Nor did Sir Nevil have much regard for the apprehensions

expressed by the more timid elements in provincial cities on the consequences should their local forces prove more militant than the 'Met'.

As far back as March he had assured the Home Office that: 'If the police of Manchester or Liverpool or Glasgow go wrong today, it would be very uncomfortable for those particular towns, but it would not shake the Empire.'

Nothing that had transpired to date had given him any cause to modify that opinion, even though in each of the areas he had named, mixed populations, appalling social conditions, industrial unrest and a strong tradition of lawlessness posed problems to their administrators that were almost unknown in London.

In fact it had always been on the cards that, in the event of a police withdrawal from their streets, all three of these great cities might well erupt in an orgy of violence that, even if it did not 'shake the Empire', would certainly shake their citizens. Yet, curiously, Macready chose to underplay this theme.

To Henri of Navarre, Paris was worth a Mass. It is possible that to Sir Nevil, though he was never to admit it, the destruction of 'political influences' in the police – influences that, he feared, could spread to the army and undermine the power of elected government – was well worth a bout of mayhem in the industrial North.

In Liverpool his philosophy would have been shared by very few.

It was hot in the packed stadium, hot both in terms of the weather and emotion. There were times when PC Petchey, of the Liverpool City Police, found the combination to be almost overwhelming.

The air was also heavy with exhortations and promises, yet somehow the longer he listened the less confident he felt that what he was hearing was altogether what the speakers pretended it to be, or even that they represented the views of those in whose name they spoke.

For here were not only police colleagues, from London and the Midlands as well as the city itself, but delegates from the radical 'triple alliance', the latter making no bones about how the dispute of their 'brothers' should be fought and won. NUPPO's sole hope of amending the coming legislation lay in strike action; strike action that should be immediate and total.

The Police Act, said a speaker for the transport workers, was aimed not only at the police comrades themselves – by suppressing the union to which they owed so much. It was also an attack against the unions as a whole and, as such, his members would support NUPPO 'to the end'. A strike by one was a strike by all.

It was heady stuff, and met with a great reception; but to Petchey and the two colleagues beside him it was also disturbing stuff, and might even be misleading.

All three were active members of the Union, but the leadership's recent – and repeated – calls for 'decisive action' had been greeted by them warily, and with puzzlement as well.

At a time when, on the grievances that had inspired the formation of the Union, the Government – under duress – had met their demands and more, it seemed odd to condemn the nation to go police-less over the question of recognition alone.

In fact for Petchey and his friends, and most other rank-and-filers, the Union existed for its members, not the other way around. And even the Union seemed of secondary importance now that the Federation was being set up in its stead.

Leonard Petchey was not the sort to preach the virtues of a servile obedience to the police authority. He had come up in the Force the hard way, and had borne – and fought against – more than his share of its traditional injustices. But neither was he the type to be carried away by a spate of fiery rhetoric. 'This liberty or death stuff' left him completely cold.

He and his colleagues had come to the meeting with no preconceived opinions as to its merits, or otherwise. Instead, they had been in a mood to listen and learn. They wanted to know how justified were these persistent threats of strike action. And they also wanted to assess how useful would be the support given to the strikers. All three were married men, and such considerations mattered.

But in Petchey's case there was an additional reason for caution: his doubts as to whether the Union's present plight arose solely from the habitual bloody-mindedness of the top brass of the police authorities or whether, in fact, it stemmed from the Union leadership's own intransigence, fuelled by the dizzy success of the previous September.

Such strokes of miscalculation as the Executive's fulsome apology for the tough police reaction to the ex-soldiers' demonstration outside the Commons — an apology that had offended PCs in every force in the country — coupled with Marston's persistent employment of fashionable Marxist phraseology, could scarcely have avoided giving offence to the most moderate of establishments: let alone the 'Prussian' Macready.

Again, like the majority of his colleagues, Petchey had hitherto considered the idea of police officers going on strike as something quite opposed to his scruples and style. Indeed, before the 1918 precedent, he would have denounced such a move as unthinkable. Nor did the ostensible response to the strike ballot do much to ease his misgivings. He was suspicious of its findings, and of its terms of reference.

The ballot's wording had been too artful, he opined: too artful by half. By mixing the recognition issue with the far more emotive question of pay and conditions of work, so that a readiness to strike on the latter point could be taken as acquiescence in strike action for the former, the authors had laid themselves open to the charge of manipulation, and the enemies of the Union had not been slow in pressing it. The ballot, so it seemed to the thoughtful Petchey, conveyed a false impression of the majority mood, and the leaders could be in danger of falling for their own propaganda.

However, as the meeting wore on, he had to agree that very few of his colleagues appeared to share his qualms.

'Let's hear what they have to say, and make up our minds accordingly,' he had said to his two companions at the start of it all; but it was clear that the majority of those present had made up their minds already. Temporarily at least, they were militants all. . . .

Positioned almost next to him was the burly form of Alec Griffin: a good copper, one of the best, yet also a NUPPO stalwart, and with strong political leanings. When Alec's turn came to speak he gave it them hot and strong.

Astutely eschewing the lofty ideological jargon that had come from certain sympathisers in other unions, he chose as his theme the way in which the police had been exploited through the decades by their masters, and their sense of public duty used as a weapon against them. He was fluent, and on a good wicket. Even Petchey found himself nodding in agreement.

Leonard Petchey had been with the police for slightly less than sixteen years – just over four years short of the minimum period then deemed necessary for a PC to have even the slightest chance of being considered for promotion.

He had joined Derby County Constabulary on 1 September 1903 and, only eight weeks later, had found himself the law's sole representative among a close-knit, inlooking tribe of tough and taciturn miners in a sprawling colliery village some miles from Sheffield. He was then nineteen years old.

The posting was a daunting one, and had caught him green and raw. Equally daunting were his new parishioners. Men scarred – and more than physically – by their bitter history, radicals with long memories and little love for bloody peelers, initially Petchey had viewed them with dismay. So too had he regarded the lack of tools for his job.

He had no telephone. Derby County was as canny as Liverpool's Watch Committee in handling its ratepayers' money. He was also, for similar reasons, denied a bicycle. When he made an arrest he had to cadge transport from his neighbours, otherwise walk the prisoner several miles to the cells in town. On one occasion he had managed to bring a drunken wife-basher to court only by pushing him there in a wheelbarrow.

Derby County had expected a lot from its young PCs. Equally, it had given them very little. For his weekly wage of £1.4.6. [£1.22½] – even tightfisted Liverpool paid its men sixpence [2½p] more – Petchey was expected to put in a minimum stint of sixty-three hours AND be on call any time of the day or night.

His lodgings had been arbitrarily chosen for him, and offered little more than a place in which to sleep. Primitive even by prevailing local standards, they appeared to have been selected not only for their cheapness but also their far remove from any source of worldly temptation. Yet in what had passed as time off, he was not allowed to leave the house without the permission of his Sergeant, to whom he had to give details of his intended whereabouts, naming also the company that he proposed to keep.

By the late summer of 1904 young Leonard felt he could stand no more of it, and said so. He resigned from the Derbyshire force on 1 August, just eleven months from the day he joined it and, shaking the coal dust from his weary feet, and slamming the door of his digs disgustedly behind him, had turned his back upon the village, never to return.

It had been Derbyshire's police authority, and not its people that had decided him to move. The local folk he had come to respect and like. 'Real decent and warm-hearted, they took a bit of knowing, but once you knew them, they presented no problem at all.'

What had knocked the youthful keenness out of Petchey had been the way in which his life had been governed by the passing whims of others: among them his unloved Sergeant, 'playing God'.

In return for a seven day week, and more, of routine labour – for the village copper there was no 'weekend' – the County had been pleased to concede him an annual dole of six days 'rest', but even this had been dependent on the Sergeant's say-so, and the latter depended entirely on the Sergeant's mood.

In eleven months, Petchey had been off-duty for only one day. Every other time he had applied for leave 'God' had – surprisingly – found his presence indispensable.

'And so much for the Good Old Days,' he now found himself reflecting. Bad days they had been, and there could be even worse. Unless, of course, you were prepared to fight for better.

The Liverpool Force, which he had joined after leaving Derbyshire, had proved to be just as exacting as its critics had always claimed. In fact, he had jumped out of the frying pan into the bloody fire. Not until recently, on being posted to the mixed suburban area of the Tue-brook, had he managed to escape from the nit-picking absurdities of the disciplines that governed a PC's lot in Liverpool Central.

The promise that had lured him to the city, of one day off a week, had vanished with the outbreak of the war. And now, by a regulation unique among those governing the country's various police forces, the local Watch Committee had refused to make this good. Liverpool businessmen could burst at the seams with the wealth they had made from the war effort. Munitions workers and dockers had trebled their take-home pay. But the copper, the Watch Committee had decided, must be prepared to 'sacrifice'. It was enough to make you spew.

With a jolt, Leonard Petchey's thoughts returned to the business of the meeting. Alec had just sat down, to record-breaking applause, and had been replaced by another speaker, this time a representative of the transport workers.

Full of fire, full of passion, and full of promise of the 'united action' that would follow any attempt to victimise the police 'should they strike in defence of their union', the new arrival was serving notice on the tyrants – both in Liverpool and Whitehall – that the old feuds that had divided the police and their fellow workers had been banished for ever. As from now they would be replaced by common unity and struggle.

'Not a wheel will turn,' he concluded, 'not a train will run, should our brothers be victimised for exerting their right to strike.'

Suddenly Petchey despaired. The fellow was talking rubbish.

'Not a wheel will turn, not a train will run.' He had not caught the identity of the speaker, and was confused over the title of his union. Could it have been the Locomotive Engineers who had so cheered the London men recently with promises of full 'supporting action'? Or could it have been the stalwarts of the Associated Society of Locomotive Engineers – the elite ASLEF – that he had so bravely pledged?

Whether the man had represented either of these two special-
ist unions, or whether he had spoken for the mass membership
NUR, embracing every aspect of the railway scene, Petchey was
never to be sure. Yet the exacting wording of the phrase
employed, and its effect upon him, was to remain razor-sharp in
his memory when other aspects of the Strike, far more dramatic,
had been buried in the years, and quite forgotten.

'Not a wheel will turn. Not a train will run.' When it came to
delivering the goods it would be a different story. It was too
much to ask for, let alone to promise. Old hatreds ran too deep.

Quite suddenly his thoughts, straying beyond the Stadium,
had anchored themselves in the city's opulent heart, just west of
Lime Street station.

And the handclaps of the conference had faded into the background, to be replaced by another, entirely different, surge of
sound: the roar of a mob and its curses, as the police charged
with batons swinging into the midst of it, and union banners,
red flags and dark blue helmets went down into the litter and the
dust. While his fellow PCs were celebrating their solidarity with
the unions, Petchey was re-living the events of eight years before,
when caught in the tragic fury of Bloody Sunday.

Dockers, transport workers and those who, simply looking for
trouble, had got much more than they had ever bargained for –
for eight years Sunday, 13 August 1911 had been hallowed by
trade unionists as a date that had made martyrs for their cause.

On the face of it, thought Petchey looking back, their strong
feelings were understandable. A monster demonstration staged
in Liverpool by the Union veteran Tom Mann had ended in
savage and bloody riot. Two men later had been shot dead
by soldiers sent to reinforce the police, and the police themselves
had reacted with a violence that had severely injured nearly a
hundred more.

Yet now the colleagues of those very same socialist 'martyrs'
were being told they must support the hated 'scuffers' whose
alleged brutality they had blamed for the rally's tragic course.
Whatever the current euphoria of the Stadium, Petchey could
feel little confidence in it lasting.

The men were being pledged by their local leaders to back those who, only yesterday, they were dubbing as 'the lackeys of the bourgeoisie', or with even more picturesque unfairness, 'The Liverpool Cossacks'. More, they were being committed to back them to their own detriment if need be. Social security for strikers, their wives and children was as yet a blessing unknown. Why take it out on the kids, for a cause that was not your own?

'Not a wheel will turn. Not a train will run . . .' It was not only PC Petchey who disbelieved in the validity of such extravagant guarantees. Disbelief was also beginning to be prevalent in the top strata of the Police Union itself.

Down in London all the powers of plausible argument commanded by Jim Hayes, all the fiery eloquence that came naturally to Joe Marston, were now being marshalled to combat it.

When, just three weeks before, he had led the NUPPO delegation to the Labour Party Conference at Southport, Marston had been greeted with a brotherly acclaim that, he professed, had almost overwhelmed him.

More, he had successfully moved a resolution whereby: 'This Conference condemns the policy of repression adopted by the Government against the National Union of Police and Prison Officers and hereby calls on the Government to grant full and frank recognition of the Union.'

But an even greater triumph, or so it seemed, was presaged by the identity of the resolution's seconder, the powerful John Bromley, general secretary of ASLEF.

A great moment for NUPPO. A great moment for Marston. Here, as their major supporter, was the key man in any decision to stop the railways in the event of the Police Strike. Nor was Bromley the only ace in the Police Union's pack.

No less a personage than Tom Mann, the arch-enemy of 1911, had demonstrated that the strength of socialist principles was greater than the divisiveness of old feuds. Brother Tom . . . Comrade Tom . . . had swung his weight behind those who had pledged themselves 'to the end' for NUPPO's cause. His influence, experience and emotional appeal would surely swing the tide.

And then, of course, they also had available the counsel of George Lansbury, dear old 'Uncle George', whose interest in their stand for the Union's recognition had never faltered since they had first announced it. Uncle George's approval and that of the *Daily Herald*, which he edited, would warm and sustain the hearts of the faithful, the political equivalent of an apostolic blessing.

When, at the end of the Conference, they had all linked hands together, and sung with brotherly fervour the words of 'The Red Flag', Marston and the other NUPPO delegates were happy men indeed. The machinations of Macready and the 'conspirators' of the Home Office had been dispelled at the first whiff of the heady Southport air, or so it seemed. Only later did the nagging doubts intrude.

Bromley, for sure, was a passionate NUPPO sympathiser: his voice had been one of the first to urge the police to strike action. But Bromley, as it slowly began to be apparent, was speaking for himself, not necessarily ASLEF's membership. He could call for a rail strike in support of the police brothers: he could not ORDER a rail strike: not on his own initiative. Under the Union's constitution his own Executive would first have to be consulted, and there was no guarantee of the nature of their reaction. Socialists all, trade union leaders could be extraordinarily conservative when it came to matters affecting the wellbeing of their members.

And then came the doubts of Mann's power to move the dockers. True that his pull was a strong one, based on affection and gratitude for past services as well as respect for current attitudes: but the powerful General Secretary of the National Union of Dock Labourers was nowadays Jimmy Sexton, and Sexton was a vastly different fish.

As one of the two Labour members on the Desborough Committee he was not only opposed to pulling out his members, should such action be required in support of the police struggle: he was also said to be opposed to the very concept of a trade union for policemen. Significantly too, there were rumours of a similar attitude spreading among his rank and file.

Examining the implications of such straws in the wind, Hayes was beginning to fidget. A realist at heart, and in that respect dissimilar to Marston, he also appreciated that fervent renderings of 'The Red Flag' at party conferences did not necessarily bind MPs to take actions that their constituents might class as 'red': party polemics and practical politics could often be poles apart.

Behind the unexpected determination of Government to implement the findings of the Desborough Committee without imposing the traditional series of historic delays, but even more in the smart decision to give an immediate cash payment to the men, Hayes could see – and give credit to – the astute manoeuvring of Macready.

Nor was the Commissioner's initiative one to be dismissed, as some would dismiss it, as mere 'bait' or, to mix metaphors, the carrot in front of the donkey. The bait was meaty. The carrot substantial. And, as an alternative to the carrot, he had made it clear that he would be ready to use the stick.

'It is to be distinctly understood by all ranks that any officer or man, of whatever rank, who fails to report in the ordinary course of duty, or when called upon, will be forthwith dismissed.'

Macready's Police Order of 30 May had now been duplicated with only slight variations of wording, by Head Constables and Watch Committees throughout the country and circulated to the borough and county forces. The bosses were getting together.

> The little tyrant's day is done
> Hurrah! Hurrah!
> See how he whimpers whines and fines
> Hurrah! Hurrah!
> Arise, Sir Premier! The Hour has come
> To press the button with your thumb
> And tell Whitehall to nip the drum.

It was all very well for the Union's *Journal* to publish poems of the calibre of this ebullient offering which, well-displayed in the current issue, caricatured the Commissioner and forecast his imminent downfall. But such rejoicings were not only premature, they could also be unwarranted, and Hayes and his colleagues knew it.

However unpopular his attributes might be to the convinced militants, Nevil Macready – his bluff approach so often masking the intent of a devious mind – was certainly not the type to 'whimper and whine'. He was determined to smash the union, and smash it he would, or else resign. His reputation, and Shortt's too, depended on his success in this objective. And reputation was vital to him.

There were times in fact when it could even be felt that the Commissioner was actually trying to force a showdown and that, far from fearing the threat of strike action, he might actually be courting it. Should the Strike be called, and then crushed, he would have rendered harmless the only weapon left in the Union's hands.

With a recent big increase in the number of fines imposed for minor disciplinary offences in the 'Met' – a move that seemed out of tune with Macready's usual style – and the increasingly overbearing attitude of the authorities in such bastions of autocracy as Liverpool and Birmingham, there was certainly sufficient colour for the 'provocation' theory to have given Hayes much scope for anxious thought.

Furthermore, it was becoming evident that, although the *Journal's* part-time poet might still repose a pathetic trust in 'Sir Premier's' goodwill towards NUPPO's cause, Lloyd George was no longer the accommodating friend he had appeared to be in that vintage September of 1918.

To 'arise' and destroy the military man he had personally chosen for Commissioner was the last thing that the Welsh Wizard would do and, to the Union Executive at least, his continuing silence in response to their appeals was making this abundantly clear.

'You can take it from me,' Marston had assured the Hyde Park rally of 1 June, 'that Lloyd George is going to clear up this mess.'

The Lloyd George method of clearance, however, could be the

63

reverse of what the Union leader had imagined.

Beset as they were by so many uncertainties, the last fortnight had been an anxious time for Hayes and the more thoughtful of his colleagues. Even the London Trades Council had shown signs of back-tracking on Carmichael's previous promises and there were reports of 'lack of sympathy' among certain London dockers, who were probably not unmindful of their difference with the police during the Dock Strike of 1912. But it was the threat posed by Desborough that continued to be the Executive's biggest headache: the Report's potential divisiveness was becoming more apparent every day.

'Take no sops of £3,' Hayes had written in the *Journal*. 'The Union is the star on which you must fix your eyes.' Only recognition he had added, with out-of-character dramatics, 'will stop Prussianised militarists from dragging in the mire free citizens of a free country.'

But just how many members would heed his words of warning? When the back-pay came through, the Act became law, and their own self-interest, plus their traditional sense of discipline, was measured against the consequences of the crunch? The 'mandate' for strike action was beginning to look rather thin.

Yet, though the Union leadership did perhaps appreciate this fact, its dilemma was cruel, and apparently inescapable. Due partly to its militancy in the past, and due also to the way in which the Home Office, under Shortt, had backed Macready's exploitation of the reaction to that militancy, the strike action it had once employed as a threat now appeared to be unavoidable. There seemed, in fact, no alternative; save for surrender and the Union's certain death.

Brutally, Shortt had privately forecast to the Premier that, given enough rope, Messrs Marston and Hayes would hang themselves. In the last week of July, they proceeded to do just that.

CHAPTER FIVE

Who Said What?

'It is to be hoped that Hayes, who was the brain behind the movement, realised the misery he had brought upon so many of his dupes and their unfortunate wives and families.'

Thus General Macready on the grim sequel to the Strike and its effect upon the men who had followed the Union's lead. Yet to others less partisan it might seem that, in sounding the call that was to cost over 2,000 police officers their careers and livelihood and bring chaos to one of Britain's greatest cities, the normally cool and purposeful Jack Hayes was acting more from desperation than from choice.

With the Police Act's passage through the Commons only days away, and with only a tiny minority of MPs opposing its provisions to ban NUPPO, the 'direct action' that had so confidently been deployed as bogeyman in the early stages of the struggle had now become the Union's only hope.

Criticism of Hayes's extravagant claims of 'big success' at the start of the strike, claims which induced many a PC who would otherwise have stayed at his post and kept out of trouble to join the action and pay for the consequences, can also be countered by a similarly pragmatic view of the circumstances prevailing at the time.

Once committed to its all-or-nothing course, it was essential for the Union to command a maximum turnout. But who would respond should the trumpet 'give forth an uncertain sound'?

Twice before had the Union been brought to the brink: each time it had thought again, recoiled and played for time. But now there was no time left, and no space in which to manoeuvre. The Union leaders must fight, or eat every word they had uttered.

So was Hayes really the shaper of events, as Macready would have us believe? Or had he found himself their helpless prisoner? The theories are conflicting, the evidence slight, it is impossible to say for certain.

The only factor that *is* certain about the tragedy which, from those last days in July, appeared to gather a fearsome momentum of its own, is that whatever their motives, and whatever their justification, both Hayes and Marston lied – and lied persistently – about the extent of support being accorded to the strike-call, and lied also about the Strike's progress and effect.

Without those lies, it could be argued, there would have been no Strike at all.

It was on Tuesday the 28th that the Union Executive, representing branches throughout the country, met in London to decide their attitude on the Strike issue and, in a spirit contradictory to the 'bolshevik' tag that had been bestowed upon them, opted for a further appeal to Lloyd George.

Unfortunately, from the moderates' point of view, the move was doomed from the start. For weeks past the Prime Minister had been in close touch with both Macready and the Home Office, and had been satisfied that the situation was very different from that of the year before. This time there would be no need to temporise with Marston and his men while the capital of the Empire went bereft of police. The Union was already a spent force and the Police Act would seal its doom.

Besides, the Welsh Wizard had other matters demanding his time and care. The bickerings among the victors of Versailles, the troubles of the White Armies in Russia, the threat of big industrial trouble on the home front and a worsening of the interminable Irish Question, all these were making heavy calls upon his magic wand. Police Strike or no, Macready and Shortt could cope. The Union delegation had been turned away at the door.

Nor had a letter from Hayes fared any better. After 'respectfully requesting' an immediate interview and an assurance that the Bill be held over until this took place, he received a reply from the Prime Minister's secretary that stated:

'Mr Lloyd George wishes me to say that, in his opinion, as the administration of the police is in the hands of the Home Secretary, you should approach Mr Shortt in this matter. In these circumstances he regrets that he is unable to comply with your request.'

This abortive attempt by the NUPPO leadership had stemmed from a factor that, carefully concealed from the membership, had confirmed the worst fears of the Hayes-Marston partnership, ready however reluctantly to implement the militancy it had so often preached.

From the moment the conference opened, the provincial representatives – with two exceptions – had made it clear that they were dead against the whole principle of a Strike, and would oppose it. 'For Marston,' in the words of one of them, 'the effect was like a blow between the teeth.'

No minutes appear to have been taken or, if they were, they were subsequently destroyed, of the proceedings of this eventful meeting, presumably one of the stormiest in the Union's troubled history.

Similarly it would appear that no written record was made of the course of the even more fateful session that followed, when the delegates had returned from their failure at Number Ten. But it would seem certain that the provincials, to judge by their subsequent actions, were still set against Strike action and that furthermore, some of the London keymen were equally opposed: certain of them going so far as to resign.

By what method these scruples were apparently over-ridden, and by what margin the decision was taken to call out the membership remains largely a mystery to this day.

And, even more mysterious, is the foundation for the subsequent claim – allegedly by Hayes – that the Executive's decision was 'unanimous' when, within hours of the Strike announcement, influential members of that 'unanimous' Executive were urging their followers to ignore the call, and continue to work as usual.

However, beset as they were by so much opposition to their plans, both Hayes and Marston must have derived considerable comfort from the fact that they continued to be supported in their stand by the two provincial stalwarts who had been in favour of strike action from the start.

So confident were Messrs Smithwick and Holliday in the militancy of their members, and so convinced that a majority of the delegates would eventually share their enthusiasm for a showdown, that they had left for home 'to call out the troops' before the vote was taken. Both were from Liverpool.

Unlike their comrades in Sheffield, blessed (to quote Mr Dobson) by a Chief Constable who was 'the finest man God ever made' . . . unlike those London PCs to whom Macready, for all his toughness, was still 'a jolly good fellow' . . . and certainly unlike their near-neighbours of the St Helens branch, soon to disaffiliate from the Union in disgust at its strike decision . . . the Liverpool men were totally out of sympathy with their uniformed superiors, let alone the local politicians on the Watch Committee, controllers of the purse-strings.

The Liverpool City Police had a long history of grievances, some of them petty, but many of them profound: grievances which the City Fathers had done nothing to put right, but on the contrary had recently exacerbated.

While his Union's Executive was still deliberating on the move that was to completely change his life, PC Tom Milburn, of Liverpool's B division was on night duty in the labyrinth of the slums that fanned out on either side of Prescot Street.

The pubs had shut. The last bit of slag had rolled home with her man. The screaming obscenities of the 'domestic incident' in Chapel Street had died into silence. A damp mist was creeping in from the sluggish Mersey, and all was quiet except for the argument in his mind.

'It's a question of socialist principle,' one part of him was urging. 'Of solidarity in a common fight.'

'A question of flouting the law, and perhaps putting yourself on the breadline,' warned the other.

With his out-thrown chest and his 'military' moustache, his slow, deliberate regulation pace and his willingness to 'mix it' with the roughs and toughs in which the area abounded, Milburn was in many respects a typical member of the unloved force, whose rough-handed rule was the only one these unhappy streets respected.

Few would have realised that, behind his traditionalist facade, Tom Milburn – PC 97 – was very much the odd man out. A sensitive dreamer and a practising socialist.

Milburn's politics stemmed from the days before he joined the force and was trying his hand at selling life insurance in West Cumberland. The misery he saw among the miners' families there had an influence that was to last him all his life.

But it was after he had enlisted in the Liverpool City Police that his sympathies hardened into strong political conviction.

Called to a tenement room in mis-named Bloom Street – 'its stink did not arise from pretty flowers' – he had been confronted by the corpse of a young woman. There was no food in the place bar a mouldy crust of bread. She had died of starvation. Next to the woman were her two small children, stunted and skeletal. They were trying to keep warm by huddling together in the heap of rags that formed their only bed. When he had first seen movement in that filthy heap, he had thought they were rats.

PC Milburn would never forget that grisly discovery, nor the sense of outrage with which he heard the coroner's verdict, delivered as if such deaths were not only commonplace but also unavoidable, so many Acts of God. To Milburn it had been murder, by a heedless and selfish society. He could see at a glance that nobody gave a damn.

Tonight, however, his thoughts were concerned with a problem quite divorced from his memory of what he had found in that squalid room, or the horrors of the twilight world encompassing his beat. He was wondering what the delegates would bring back from London, and, even more urgently, just how he would react to what they brought.

When you had a wife to keep and two children under five, the Liverpool City Police Force was no bed of roses.

At the time he joined, in 1912, the contents of Milburn's weekly pay-packet had averaged, after deductions, £1.4.5.

[£1.22] or somewhat less than that of a dockers' labourer, but he had consoled himself with the thought that he would have the right to a pension.

Six years later, his position had worsened considerably. While his own wage had risen to £1.10.0. [£1.50] plus a war bonus of eight shillings [40p] the labourer's had shot up to £3.6.9. [£3.35] and the pension's value had been halved by wartime inflation.

There were many disadvantages for those serving the law on Merseyside, and very little chance of doing anything to remedy them. Deprived of industrial muscle, by the absence of a union, and denied negotiating machinery through which they could plead their cause, the troubles of the police had gone unheeded.

In any city where crime and sectarianism exist on a massive scale, where there are extremes of wealth and poverty, with little in between, and where a mixture of races provides additional fuel for conflict, it is probably inevitable that the policing should be harsh, bearing heavily on any threat to the *status quo*.

Equally inevitable is the tendency to apply harsh measures inside the force itself, but the discipline practised in Liverpool was so extreme as to be almost legendary, and part-farcical as well.

On one occasion Milburn had been paraded before the Area Superintendent, for standing on the platform of a tram when there were inside seats available. He had done so to prevent the rain running down his cape from inconveniencing other passengers, but his explanation had not been well received. The Superintendent had taken the view that he had failed to act with the dignity becoming a member of the force: 'It might have been thought that you were trying to dodge paying the fare.'

Such a niggling attention to the trivial was characteristic of the attitudes adopted towards humble PCs by those placed in authority over them in the Liverpool area.

Only recently, Milburn had experienced yet another example of the type of thinking that contributed to this process when, having returned home dead-weary after night-shift, he had been roused from bed and ordered to report back to the station.

It transpired that the Station Sergeant had failed to hear him utter the customary 'All Correct' when signing off and, instead of querying the matter then and there, had waited for him to go home, so as to recall him to repeat the words as punishment.

'I'd like to have punched the small-minded bastard,' Milburn said. 'But of course, I didn't . . .'

There was no way a PC could appeal against such irritants. He was expected to suffer in silence: it was part of a policeman's lot. Nor was there any way in which redress could be obtained for the financial hardship inflicted on him by the Watch Committee's obsessive preoccupation with economies.

Even now, despite the Government's measures to improve the lot of the police forces in general, the Liverpool men were badly underprivileged.

Predictably the Watch Committee, under the chairmanship of the massively built – and massively prejudiced – Alderman Maxwell, had sought consistently to break the power of the Union. But what had really made the local men see red was when it also refused to allow the 'representative Boards to speak for the rank and file' that the Government had approved under the 1918 settlement.

'No other group of workers would have been subjected to such repressive treatment, yet the police, because of their non-alignment with the parties, were expected to say nothing, and obey,' Milburn was to recall in later years.

Nor would the Watch Committee, and this was a particularly sore point with the married men, grant pay or time off for the 'rest days' the police had worked throughout the war. Regardless of the Government's advice, and Macready's example, Maxwell and his colleagues had turned the idea down flat.

'But it's OUR money. We've been robbed!' Milburn had protested.

'They've robbed us through the decades,' his Branch Secretary had replied. 'But wait and see, it'll be different soon.'

Tom Milburn hoped he was right, but he could not help but wonder. In fact he was wondering now: how soon would be the 'soon'?

To make ends meet, and keep home and family together

during the past four years of soaring prices he had been forced to take jobs on the side in his all too scant spare-time.

Keeping the queues in order outside the old Olympia and Hippodrome . . . sweating out each Sunday on a farm . . . volunteering for night patrols with the mounted force, his only chance of 'official' overtime . . . Milburn, in his efforts for his family, had worked every hour God gave him and it still had not been enough. Yet now he was likely to be asked to put everything to risk. The wife, the kids, his career, at the summons of the Union.

A question of socialist principles, to answer the call to strike? It really was not so simple as that, and surely the leaders must know it.

Milburn had joined the National Union of Police and Prison Officers back in 1916, when to be a known member, or even a sympathiser was to court heavy fines, and very often the sack. Yet though liable to be subjected to the most irritating provocations, and forced to confine their meetings to secret sessions in each other's homes, neither he nor his PC colleagues had ever contemplated anything so revolutionary as a strike.

In fact, the Union's founders had specifically barred strike action from its members and only since Marston's revision of the rules had it been possible for the new leadership to call for this final sanction. To many dedicated Union members strike action was still anathema.

It was also near-anathema to Milburn and for this, paradoxically, the socialist in him was probably responsible.

The PC's sense of compassion for his 'parish' and parishioners was sincere, and deeply rooted. But he allowed himself very few illusions over what would happen to these victims of the 'system' should the 'system' disappear overnight.

For the police to withdraw their services would be no way to the millennium. Razor gangs, cutpurses, pickpockets, pimps and prostitutes, these would be the characters who would rule the streets in their absence; and rule them with a tyranny far worse than anything the meanest-minded scuffer could impose. Once the Law withdrew, anarchy would take over, and *then* God help the working classes, thought Tom Milburn, for no one else would.

On the other side of the coin, however, was the question of loyalty to one's mates — fellow coppers, fellow scuffers, fellow members of a Union, fighting for its life. He as an individual was dead against strike action: but who was he to stand against the many? Collective action. Collective responsibility. Was not that what a union was supposed to be about?

He came to his decision just before the ending of the shift. It was not a clear cut-decision, but a compromise with conscience.

He would wait and see what the lads had to say about it: when they'd heard what London was doing, and how the executive felt. Could be that, after all, a strike would not be called for, and that Government and Union might reach a compromise. But if it was, and the others wanted it, then he would not be odd man out. He would back them despite his own feelings. It was a question of honour.

So what *did* the lads have to say about it? The Union leaders allowed small scope for rank-and-file discussions. 'Dilly-dally'on the part of the Home Office might indeed have been responsible for the Government's crushing defeat in September 1918, but nobody could accuse Hayes and Marston of allowing the Union to indulge a similar fault. The decision to go ahead with the National Strike was reached by the executive on Wednesday 29th. No time was lost in implementing it.

A mass meeting of members was called for the following evening at the Central Hall, Commercial Road, Stepney, where they were told that the Strike would be effective that very same night: starting at ten o'clock.

Ostensibly to shield members from subsequent victimisation, the meeting was private and the Press was excluded: though it is probable that the well-disposed *Daily Herald's* description of applause that greeted the decision as 'indescribable' owed more to its author's devotion to superlatives rather than the effectiveness of censorship.

Indeed, the *Herald* could be said to have had an extra territorial status in Stepney that night, with its editor George

Lansbury addressing the meeting and not only approving the decision to strike but saying that he would not have been there had the strike NOT been declared.

Now they were 'out' he urged every man and woman to stand by each other to the bitter end.

The unhappy choice of adjective was lost in a storm of applause.

Once proceedings were concluded and 'Uncle George' had returned in haste to his newspaper, to prepare what was to be a historic first edition scoop, the leadership proved ready and willing enough to project its views to the rest of the Press, far less sympathetic than the *Herald* to its cause – and thence to members as yet unaware of what had been done in their name and the action expected of them.

Significantly, Marston – in talking to the Press – was particularly severe in criticising the Police Bill's provisions for the formation of the Police Federation. 'This unjust legislation,' he demanded 'must be withdrawn without delay.'

And the *Daily Mirror*, quoting the views of other union leaders reported to its readers that 'especially do they object to the Government scheme of representation for the whole of the police force of the country, whereby it is stated that every policeman will be called on to withdraw from his union with the alternative of dismissal from the service.'

To the leader-writer of *The Times*, however, the dismissal penalty could not come fast enough. In the course of a portentous denunciation of 'these fomentors of disorder' he promised that 'the public will support the police authorities in visiting upon the defenders the punishment they have deserved.' In Printing House Square, they gave short shrift to strikers.

What neither the *Mirror*, nor *The Times*, nor indeed any other national newspaper thought fit to comment upon, was the almost total absence of representatives from the provinces among the crowd that spilled into the Commercial Road at the conclusion of the meeting. In fact it is possible that their absence had not even been noticed. When reduced to civilian clothes, and without the differences in helmet shape, badges and numerals that distinguished the separate forces, the policeman of one area could look very much like his colleague in another, and few Fleet Street journalists would have been acquainted with Union personalities outside the London area.

Again, as Hayes had already taken the precaution of jauntily assuring fellow unionists that the provincial comrades were already on their way home to 'call out their troops', even a reporter well-informed enough to have spotted the gaps in the ranks of the faithful would scarcely have appreciated their real significance.

As it was, however, this failure to note, and evaluate, the shattering silence from the provinces was to exert a powerful influence upon the whole progress of events.

The authority of the platform to speak as the united voice of the Union's Executive was left unchallenged, and its emphasis on 'united action', as published in the papers the following morning, acquired an authenticity that was to induce many who would otherwise have plumbed for more moderate courses to follow its militant lead.

Nor was the Executive slow in seizing on the opportunity afforded it by the media to reach a wider audience than the Police Union itself.

In a statement that bore the unmistakable stamp of Jim Hayes, it attacked the Government's attitude to NUPPO as part of 'a general harassment of the trade union movement as a whole'. It promised 'a call to all sections of organised labour' to rally to the support of the Strike.

Additionally, it pledged a series of demonstrations by the Metropolitan and City Police Forces for the following day: among them a rally on Tower Hill and a protest march on Downing Street.

It was confident stuff, without a hint of the deep divisions on policy that had cut through the once united front of the Union's leadership. And, in their promise of producing 'immediate action', the militants were even better than their word.

Scarcely had the meeting dispersed than a fleet of taxicabs carrying Union officials and plastered with posters bearing the message 'Police Strike Tonight' began to tour the streets of the East End, calling on every police station in the area. It was an initiative that, initially, appeared to achieve a big success.

In H Division it was reported that many of the men on duty left their beats as soon as they heard the news, withdrawing in advance of the Strike deadline, while those reporting for the 10pm shift promptly went home again.

At Bethnal Green police station a handful of officers decided to defy the call, claiming there was no justification for striking on the recognition issue alone. But this protest notwithstanding, the bulk of the night shift was won over by the eloquence of a visiting Union official, and by midnight they too were voting with their feet.

For East Ham it was a very similar story. Within an hour of a picket line being established only the station's administrative staff remained at work.

It was true that not every area was so quick to embrace the Strike. Reporters sent to assess the strength of support for the strike call found the police in the West End functioning 'pretty well the same as usual'.

A number of uniformed men were controlling the theatre crowds at the Opera House, Covent Garden and, unlike the situation that had followed the Strike order of 1918, there appeared to be no mass defections from the Central area. In Whitehall the government offices continued to be defended by the men of Z Division, and this time the forecourt of the Yard was untouched by demonstrations of revolt.

Press enquiries in the City yielded even more surprises. The night shift had reported for duty and by the time the papers went to press only one of the City of London Police Force's 1,900 members had withdrawn his labour. And *he* was a Sergeant Zoller, a leading light of the Union's Executive and a man long renowned for the militancy of his political views.

But however poor the response to the Strike call in the City, and however patchy the situation in the Metropolitan divisions, it was noticeable that on the streets of the capital as a whole, there were far fewer police on duty than there were the night before.

Again, as the Strike leaders were naturally quick to point out, only a comparatively small number of their members were as yet aware of the call: an ignorance that the *Daily Herald* was doing its best to remedy.

On the *Herald* night desk they were working at top speed to bring out a special edition on the Strike: an edition that carried the Strike Manifesto handed to it in advance of Marston's statement.

Thanks to George Lansbury's foreknowledge of the Strike decision, they had their 'scoop' and would make the most of it.

By the following morning Labour sympathisers throughout the country would be reading the Manifesto's text in full; and, hopefully, rally to its support. The text opened with the phrase: 'You Must Act Now, or lose your freedom for ever.'

You must act now, or lose your freedom for ever. Your executive committee has, therefore, decided upon making use of the final argument and this statement should be accepted as official notification that members of the National Union of Police and Prison Officers withdraw their services immediately, such withdrawal to remain effective until the gross injustices imposed by the provisions of Sections 1, 2 and 3 of the Police Bill are remedied, and full and frank recognition of your Union is conceded. The members of your executive committee have already withdrawn their services, and are prepared to sacrifice all for the cause, being assured that the members they represent will fight for justice and liberty, with determination second to none.

It was a brave and defiant document, admitting no compromise. It was a statement to put fire into the stomachs of the craven and shame the arguments of the stubborn individualist objector. It was also, as events were to prove, extraordinarily contentious in its treatment of the facts.

The picture it projected, of an Executive Committee united in purpose and action, was an inspiring one, providing a model for the rank and file to follow. But unfortunately for the rank and file who did so this portrait of harmonious resolve was not only over-coloured and unbalanced in its perspective: it was also not drawn from life. The scene it portrayed did not exist.

Even as the *Herald's* presses began their mass-publication of the leadership's call to arms, the hitherto solid ranks of the National Union of Police and Prison Officers were beginning to split apart.

Men who had fought together for the Union since the time of its inception were at the start of a great divide. It was one that, never to be closed, would leave a legacy of bitterness between old comrades for decades to come. Some Executive members would indeed be ready to 'sacrifice all for the cause' and call upon their followers to rally to the Strike: but others would be calling upon theirs to stand firm and defy it.

In London, several of those who had been prominent in their support for the Strike of 1918 were among the latter, and had already planned meetings in which they would assail the current use of this 'the final argument' as completely unrepresentative of the majority feeling.

Meanwhile, the provincial members of the 'united' Executive Committee were travelling home as fast as the rails could carry them, not to 'call out their troops', as Hayes pretended, but to restrain their members from following the Manifesto's lead!

In Liverpool, however, they were sublimely unaware of these developments, and had no concept at all of the disagreement that was to tear the Union in two. The city's militant delegates – Constables Holliday and Smithwick – who had so emphatically backed the hardline at Wednesday's session of the Executive Committee, had talked of nothing since their return but the inevitability of a Strike decision, and the need for the Merseyside force to show solidarity with the rest of their brethren by a massive response to make the Strike effective. This, the Liverpool men, smarting under their own impressive set of grievances, were in a ready mood to do.

To allow young police recruit John Ford a break from lectures and textbooks and offer him, instead, 'a taste of the real thing', he had been posted to Essex Street (C Division) placed under the care of a serving Constable and then sent on a three hour spell of street duty.

It was an interesting evening, though not particularly eventful, and it was not until he returned to the station that anything unusual occurred.

Finding he had a few minutes to wait before dismissal, he started to glance through the Head Constable's Order Book, referring to the bank holiday arrangements for traffic duty at the Landing Stage.

To his astonishment, a veteran 'regular' then nearing the end of his service, grabbed the book from his hands, slammed the pages shut and firmly replaced it on the desk.

'Nobody will be doing that duty,' the man said grimly.

'I beg your pardon? What's the trouble?'

'You'll learn time enough . . .'

It was not until the following morning that Ford realised the full significance of the incident. The Landing Stage would be bereft of police for days to come.

The spark that lit the fuse of the Liverpool explosion came in the form of a telegram from Hayes. It said simply:
'STRIKE DECLARED. OVER THE TOP. BEST OF LUCK.'

Immediately the call-out machinery that the local branch of the Union had been preparing for the past month went into motion with, as in London, a lavish employment of taxi-cabs bedecked with placards, some of the latter having originally been manufactured for the Strike call anticipated for 29 June and kept in store since its postponement.

But, and here the Liverpool militants had the advantage over their counterparts in the Metropolitan area, not only was the branch leadership unanimous in its lack of misgivings over the wisdom of the Strike but, owing to the smaller size of the force, had a much tighter grip upon its membership.

Over the past year a vigorous recruiting campaign had resulted in nearly eighty per cent of Liverpool's policemen joining the Union, and as these were concentrated for the most part in the central areas of the city, they were readily accessible to the Strike Committee's control.

Paradoxically, the unique sense of comradeship that had been forged among the lower ranks during the violence of Bloody Sunday and similar affrays when they had clashed with the legions of organised labour was also a factor that, in this instance, worked favourably for the Union.

When fellow PCs had been exposed to attack, the men of the Liverpool force had seldom bothered overmuch about the identity or the motives of the attackers. They had gone straight at them.

Working-class demonstrators . . . sectarian rioters . . . criminal thugs, equipped with razor or cosh . . . all categories of the city's abundant trouble-makers had experienced the crushing strength of the 'scuffers' reaction.

And the fact that this current attack came not from 'radicals' but the Government made little difference to the force's traditional response: one of immediate assistance when a comrade called for help.

As yet, despite the activity in the streets, where PCs reporting for duty had been intercepted by the pickets and sent home, and others had been ordered off point-duty or their beats, the civilian community was unaware of what was happening to its guardians. Tomorrow it was going to have a hell of a shock.

CHAPTER SIX

A 'Herald' at Lime Street

It was early morning on Friday 1 August when a group of men in well-brushed civilian clothes stepped smartly through the entrance to Lime Street Station that led from St George's Square and positioned themselves outside the platform barrier, to wait for the arrival of the overnight train from London.

With their straw hats anchored squarely on short and tidy haircuts, and their square-toed boots glistening with polish, the newcomers certainly made an odd contrast to the 'regulars' frequenting the place at this wan time of the day. The railway policeman on duty regarded them with more than usual interest.

He had encountered one or two of the men before, though at first he found it difficult to recognise them. They looked so different, now they were out of uniform. But, viewed in the group, their calling was unmistakable.

'Bloody scuffers,' the meths-soaked old tramp, lying in the unswept little yard outside the Gents, snarled spitefully. 'You can tell 'em a mile off, the bastards!'

So what were the City Police up to now the PC wondered?

'Thought we'd get an early look at the morning papers,' said one of them, adding with a grin at the surprised expression: 'We're waiting to hear how the Met has responded to the strike call. Should be a record turnout, so we're told.'

He himself, he confided, had been unaware that the action was imminent until, on his way to report for duty, he had heard the repeated blasts of a police whistle. Expecting 'a fine old barney' as he put it, he had rushed to the source of the sound, only to find it was a ploy by union pickets to get the members together and pass on orders to strike.

When, a little peeved at the way the news had been broken, he had asked how popular the Strike was likely to be elsewhere, he had got the short answer: 'Our colleagues are already out in strength, as you'll see from this morning's *Herald*. They're doing fine.'

Now he, along with others of his shift, had come to meet the paper train and see if the *Daily Herald* really had such goodies to offer: 'We'll believe it when we see it in black and white.'

However, ten minutes later, the picket's forecast of the *Herald's* contents was shown to have been remarkably accurate. In fact, if it erred at all, it was through understatement.

'You Must Act Now, or lose your freedom for ever,' the words of the Manifesto were splashed boldly across the paper's front and flanked by enthusiastic reports of a massive walkout.

'London Police defy the Government', was the headline that set the tone of the paper's impressions of the Metropolitan scene.

Very few PCs were to be seen on the streets, and there was talk of other unions rallying to NUPPO's support. Marston and Hayes were claiming 'a big success'.

Reassured by the results of their research, the men walked out of the station and then, in compliance with the Union's orders, instead of going on duty they all went home.

If Londoners could do what they were doing, the lads from Liverpool would not be slow in following suit.

When the City Fathers came to tot up the tally of ruin that the withdrawal of its defenders had cost the city they were reported as saying that the Police Strike had been a complete surprise to them. They had no 'inkling' there was discontent within the force.

Had there been a competition for the most incredible of the many incredible statements put out by the opposing parties in the crisis, this, surely, would have taken the prize.

What, for example, had the Head Constable and the Watch Committee deduced from the extraordinary fact that, while the official 'returns', prepared fortnightly, normally listed two or three resignations over the period, in the week leading up to

the 'mutiny' no fewer than one Superintendent, seventeen Inspectors forty-nine Sergeants and sixty-eight Constables had
suddenly decided to quit the force?

Did no one in authority see in this sudden exodus, fears of
trouble to come? And associate the resignations with the action
of men anxious to preserve their pension rights?

And then there was the odd phenomenon whereby – at a time
of massive unemployment – Liverpool had found it difficult to
attract recruits.

In taking his aggressive stance against the Union, one of
Macready's top cards had been the long waiting list of entrants
for the Metropolitan Police. Gaps in the ranks caused by dismissals could quickly be made good.

But in Liverpool, during the months preceding the strike,
there had been no such glut of eager applicants, although since
the announcement of the Desborough Award, a modest intake of
some sixty young recruits promised to ease a little the problems
posed by the force's acute undermanning.

Most of these men were ex-soldiers, recently demobbed, and as
it happened they were to play a part in the city's troubles that
was to be entirely disproportionate to their numbers. Gerald
O'Keeffe was one of them.

O'Keeffe had joined the ranks of the Liverpool City Police on 1
July and so far had failed to find the service as oppressive as he
had been told. A single man, he had no gripe about the pay; not
now that the new rate was on the way. A trainee, he had no
Union ties, and therefore, no clash of loyalties arose between his
duty to the Union and the public. And, after the misery of the
trenches, even the needling received from the police NCOs
proved not impossible to bear. In comparison with Flanders it
was almost a piece of cake.

When O'Keeffe awoke on Friday morning, and started to get
himself spruced up to report to Police HQ he had not the faintest
idea that there was anything about the day that would distinguish it from any other in the working week.

The recruits had been so isolated from the serving veterans

that few of them appreciated that a Police Union existed, let alone that it was proceeding towards a head-on collision with Government. That morning their ignorance seemed shared by the populace as a whole.

Apart from neighbours' gossip about calls made on the homes of certain serving policemen during the night, and rumours about a commotion around the Central Fire Station, where strikers in plain clothes had endeavoured to call out the firemen, little was known to the workers who crammed the early morning trams about the crisis that was to convulse the city.

Even the *Herald's* strident summary of events failed to make its local readers much the wiser. The action it portrayed was taking place down in London, and made little personal impact. Only the *Liverpool Daily Post* served to draw attention to the possibility that this Police Strike, unlike its predecessor, would have repercussions much nearer home.

The *Post* had reported that 'elements' in the Liverpool City Police Force had withdrawn their services in support of NUPPO's stand. No police were to be seen on point-duty in the main shopping and business sectors and the police guards had been withdrawn from the landing stages on the Mersey. The local Strike Committee had announced a meeting of union members, to be held that same evening in St George's Hall.

However, even the *Post's* report on the progress of the dispute did not unduly disturb the early risers, regarding it with mild interest rather than alarm, while O'Keeffe for one, had not even seen the paper. Always the good soldier, he had been far too busy polishing his buttons.

It was so good to escape the humiliations of the Labour Exchange, and find himself in a uniform again, even though one with a different cut and colour to the old Khaki serge: that applying the metal polish, he had burst into snatches of song. It was good, too, to present a smart appearance to the foe and though, in this instance, the 'foe' was no more substantial a menace than his Training Sergeant, O'Keeffe was not one to plead circumstance as a reason for departing from a principle. The morning of 1 August had found him a happy man.

It was not until he and his mate — fellow-recruit John Harrison — were walking down William Brown Street on their way to 'The Garden', that they heard the news. But it took a minute or two for them to digest it, and realise that it could involve them personally.

A man in civvies had approached them, and introduced himself as a Sergeant, attached to Seel Street.

'You must go back home,' he said, 'or help on the picket line. We're all on strike.'

'What the hell has that got to do with *us?*' asked Gerald O'Keeffe, astonished.

'Union orders . . .'

'We've no complaints,' he protested. 'We're not even Union members.'

The Sergeant smiled grimly: 'Don't worry about that. We can settle *that* little problem as quickly as Jack Robinson. I can make both of you members on the spot.'

Union members? When they knew nothing about unions, and even less about the strike? 'His offer,' O'Keeffe was to recall, 'seemed, on the face of it, a bit naïve.'

Thanking the Sergeant for putting them in the picture, but politely refraining from committing themselves, the two decided the best thing for them to do was to proceed as planned to Hatton Garden.

'There'll probably be pickets who will do their best to stop us,' Harrison warned. 'But at least we'll know what's up, and what this business is all about.'

'About bloody time too,' O'Keeffe replied.

One man at least knew what the Strike was all about: Lieutenant-General Sir Nevil Macready, installed in his HQ at Scotland Yard for the 'duration', and evidently enjoying it.

Anticipating as he had that Marston and Hayes must eventually 'go over the top' he had already briefed his senior officers — in the light of his own careful study of the 1918 crisis — on the probable course the strike would take, and the tactics of the strikers.

And he had also drawn the attention of his audience to the concluding paragraph of the Police Order of 30 March: 'Officers and men will, if necessary, defend themselves by all means if interfered with in the execution of their duty.'

This time, attempts to intimidate non-strikers would be firmly met.

When the Union Executive at last reached their decision it therefore caused little surprise in the top echelons of the Yard, and failed to ruffle even the surface composure of the Commissioner when telephoned by his deputy while at a dinner party in the Commons.

'Sealed orders had been sent out to all divisions,' he subsequently recorded in his memoirs, 'to be opened on receipt of telegraphic or telephonic code words, and Sir Edward Ward had been notified that his Special Constabulary might be required in strength at short notice.'

Sir William Nott-Bower, Commissioner of the City Police, had also been informed of the steps that the 'Met' would take against the strikers. Liaison between the two forces had never been closer.

In fact, so confident did Macready feel in the adequacy of his plans that, 'not wishing to spread alarm and despondency (a military phrase!) among our legislators,' he dallied over the dinner table for another hour before returning to Scotland Yard, where the Assistant Commissioner, General Sir William Horwood, his own nominee, had been commanding in his absence. Things were as well as could be.

At risk of giving an impression to outside observers that support for the Strike was stronger than it really was, Macready had ruled that, initially, men reporting for duty should be kept inside their stations instead of being sent on their normal beats.

This, as he saw it, would fulfil a threefold purpose. It would confuse the militants as to the strength, or otherwise, of their following. It would protect the stations against take-over attempts. And it would avoid situations — so commonplace during the previous affair — where individual PCs were pressurised by roaming pickets.

TOP: **'Prussian' at the Yard**

eneral the Rt. Hon. Sir Nevil Macready Bart., G.C.M.G., K.C.B. swaps khaki for
ıe, as Commissioner of the Metropolitan Police Force. *Radio Times Hulton Picture
Library.*

BELOW: **'Bolshevik' on Tower Hill**

-Police Sgt Jack Hayes, secretary of the 'unrecognised' Police Union addresses the
union's faithful. *Daily Herald.*

LATE LONDON EDITION

DAILY HERALD

NO. 1,099 (No. 106—New Series)   LONDON, FRIDAY, AUGUST 1, 1919.   ONE PENNY.

LONDON POLICE DEFY THE GOVERNMENT

SURPRISE POLICE STRIKE

Dramatic Result of Government's Attempt to Suppress a Trade Union

LONDON FORCE OUT LAST NIGHT

West-End Traffic Left to Look After Itself; Crowd Congratulates Homeward-Bound Constables

A surprise police strike began in London last night. It is expected to spread throughout the country to-day.

Enthusiastic mass meetings of members of the Police Union, in response to appeals from their Executive, decided on a strike forthwith for recognition of the Union.

Few police constables were on duty in the Metropolis last night, and those that were had not been acquainted with the strike decision.

The police have been forced to take this step because of the deliberate attempt by the Government, through the Police Bill, to deprive them of their Unions. Under the clauses of that Bill not only are policemen forbidden to join a Union of their own, not only are they forbidden to have anything to do with the Labour movement, but heavy penalties are to be inflicted on anyone attempting to organise the police or in any way causing disaffection.

Any such person is to be liable, under Clause 3, to imprisonment, with or without hard labour, for a term not exceeding two years, or to a fine on summary conviction, or to both fine and imprisonment.

The Police and Prison Officers' Union regards this Bill as an attack not only upon them, but upon the whole of Labour.

POLICE HANG UP TRUNCHEONS

Mass Meeting Last Night Declares for General Strike

A strike decision was reached at an enthusiastic and largely attended meeting of the London Police Union, and held in the Central Hall, Commercial road E., when the officers of the Union discussed the men.

Mr. J. L. Marston, president of the Union, who presided, and was loudly cheered, said:—

"Your Executive Committee, representing every part of the United Kingdom, met yesterday and came to the conclusion we had to fight to live—cheerily or else give up the fight. (Loud cries of 'Never!')

"We might have taken direct action yesterday. In deference to some of your comrades, and in order to meet as far as possible the wishes of those in favour of what is termed constitutional methods, direct action was deferred."

At a late hour last night a deputation of the executive waited on Mr. Lloyd George to ask that the Police Bill, at sections 1, 2, and 3, be held over until such time as the interview could be given.

It was also decided to also for full and frank recognition of the National Union. (Cheers.)

The Prime Minister's private secretary asked peremptorily the deputation the slightest communication with the Prime Minister.

The Executive Committee sat again, until it was resolved that they must fight. (Loud cheers and voices " Do we start now?")

The whole of the Executive Committee were at that moment in session. (Cheers.)

"I am now taking your instructions of every hero—that you are now on strike." (An indescribable scene of enthusiasm followed.)

"Your comrades of the Provincial Executive hurriedly left at noon to-day, to get out their own men." (Loud cheers.)

NATIONAL STRIKE AT ONCE

Police and Prison Service Reply to Government Bill

The following manifesto, "To all Police and Prison Officers in Great Britain and Ireland," is issued by the Executive of the Police Union through the " Daily Herald ":—

The Government has dared to persist in its effort to utilise political machinery to destroy your constitutional right to organise for the legal protection of your own interests.

The preservation of your Union and the future welfare of your wives and children wholly depend upon the full exercise of the power of your own organisation. They power at the only means by which you can retain your hard won freedom as citizens. If and when your conciliatory efforts are ignored by the authorities.

The Police Bill now before Parliament will, in its very near future, become law, and the passage of this measure will mean the complete destruction of your Union—the existence of which was fully agreed to by the Prime Minister on August 27, 1918, and again by Lord Cave on behalf of the Government on September 12, 1918.

Peaceful Methods Fail

Every possible constitutional and pacific channel has been traversed in order to arrive at a satisfactory solution.

A final explanation of the position, together with an application for an interview, was carried to the Prime Minister at 10, Downing street, at 11 p.m. on July 30, 1919, and again at 10 a.m. on July 31, by a deputation of your Executive Committee, elected for that purpose, who waited for a reply.

Even this procedure has been ignored.

Therefore you are driven to the final argument: "You must act or lose your freedom for ever."

Your Executive Committee has, therefore, decided upon making one of the final argument, and this statement should be accepted as the official notification that members of this National Union of Police and Prison Officers WITHDRAW THEIR SERVICES IMMEDIATELY, such withdrawal to remain effective until the gross injustices imposed by the provisions of Section 1, 11, and 111 of the Police Bill are removed, and full and frank recognition of our Union is secured.

The members of your Executive Committee have already withdrawn their services, and are prepared to sacrifice all for the cause, being assured that the numbers they represent will fight for justice and liberty, with determination second to none.

(Signed) J. H. HAYES,
General Secretary.

EXCITEMENT IN THE WEST END

Hawkers Do a Roaring Trade Without " Moving On "

WOMEN AS PICKETS

With dramatic suddenness London police struck last night.

They left their beats quickly and without demonstration, each district rejoicing as the news came through that their comrades elsewhere were supporting them.

The startling feature was the unanimity of the men : their resolve.

The West End (writes a DAILY HERALD representative), though missing the familiar figures of the policemen on point duty, did not realise that a police strike had actually started, till nearly 10 p.m.

The late fruit hawkers, who are generally kept on the move, got the news early, and took full advantage of it to carry on their trade undisturbed.

Among the theatre crowds in Leicester square, one lone policeman, homeward bound, was asked on all sides whether the police were really on strike, and when he confirmed the news he was patted on the back and shaken hands with by the sympathetic crowd.

At Piccadilly corner, one policeman, in his excitement at hearing the news, burned off, leaving his truncheon hanging on a post at the shelter.

A feature of the strike is the proposed employment of women pickets. The women who drew up these pickets are to cover cases who, having volunteered their services.

East End's Escape

Taxicabs toured the East End, and in a very short time the strike was general in Bethnal Green, Hackney, Stepney, Whitechapel, Limehouse, and Poplar.

East Ham quickly followed, as did Shoreditch.

Not was need parted from east in this case, the men of Gerrard row, within the precincts of the Palace of Westminster, and all answered the call when it came.

PREMIER BREAKS PLEDGE

INTERVIEW WITH UNION REFUSED

The following is a copy of the correspondence with the Prime Minister this week which has compelled the executive of the Police Union to order the strike:—

POLICE UNION to PREMIER, July 30, 1919.

Sir,—I am directed by my Executive Committee to request an interview with you that they are now contemplating necessary to be taken by them effectively to oppose the adoption of Sections 1, 2, and 3 of the Police Bill, which in being rushed to Parliament as of sudden drive; and I am respectfully to request an immediate interview to be granted to a deputation of this E.C. to represent the feelings of the Police authorities in regard to this portion of this serious business.

This urgent request is made in the earnest hope that judgment may be conceded with the time-honoured principles of the Government, namely that, as we have no intention of legislation in matters affecting the interests of their home, without due recognition and the full consideration of all phases of our side.—I am, your obedient servant, and Lord Cave on August 3, and September 12 respectively.

I cannot too earnestly impress upon you, sir, the grave nature of the present situation, and it is with the utmost desire to find a conciliatory compromise out of the present difficulty that this appeal is made to you. We also have had regard to the interest of the community in general.—J. HAYES, General Secretary.

The Premier's Reply

This letter was handed in at 10, Downing street, by the deputation from the Executive Committee of the Union.

In spite of the Prime Minister's specific directions last August that the Police Union should communicate with him at any time there was any serious difficulty, the following answer was handed to the waiting deputation.

PREMIER'S SECRETARY to the UNION, July 31, 1919.

Dear Sir,—I am desired by the Prime Minister to acknowledge the receipt of your letter of the 30th inst. in regard to the proposal by the Police Union to oppose the passage of the Police Bill now before the House of Commons.

Mr. Lloyd George wishes me to say that, as he opinion on the administration of the Police is in the hands of the Home Secretary, you should approach Mr. Short in this matter.

Under the circumstances, he regrets that he is unable to comply with your request. Yours faithfully,

HOW AND WHERE THEY CAME OUT

Royal Performance at Opera Left Without Constables

Popular men are all out.
Constable Speakman was almost idolised by his comrades.

Strike Committees were formed in each district to arrange picketing.

Many women, as enthusiastic as the men, attended yesterday's mass meetings.

The police will hold a demonstration on Tower Hill this morning at 10 o'clock.

There were something like 60,000 P.C.'s and prison officials out on strike last night.

Only two or three constables remained on duty at East Ham Police Station last night.

"It's not money we are after, but freedom," said Tommy Thiel, the organising secretary.

The City men are entitled to draw their pay to-day. Some are remaining till they get withdrawn.

Officers on duty at the Opera last night, on the occasion of the visit of Royalty, were withdrawn.

Highbury men were active early last night in getting away from duty. They must be on the telephone!

"God help those remaining when I get at them," said the wife of a P.C. who is one after 21 years' service.

No Price Too High

" No Price Too High when Honour is at Stake " was the bill shown at one meeting. The author is the Premier!

A sergeant in the Metropolitan Force said last night that he would leave at once if the Police Bill became law.

Where policemen are figuring in cases, they are giving evidence after informing the magistrate they are on strike.

" All the 875 men of my branch are to be counted on to stand by their comrades."—Mr. Lawson, of Hammersmith.

East London men on night duty, who had been asleep during the day, waited eagerly for the pickets to rouse them to 'push up.'

There is an order in force by the Commissioner to the effect that no curfew will be taken if a constable does bad service for duty.

Don't trifle in any shape or form with authority during our present conflict.—Mr. Marston, president of the Union, to policemen last night.

" I had an order to present myself to General Macready this morning," declared an Inspector last night. " But it can't be done—I'm out of work."

" After 25 years' service I would rather get the sack," said one striker, " than live under such conditions as that the Police Bill would bring to us."

At all branch meetings of the Police Union last night resolutions were passed pledging the police to oppose the Government's attempt to crush the Union.

are they? are Want?

Sir Edward Ward said last night : " The men have got everything they want. It is ridiculous to suggest that they will denationalise themselves with any strike."

" My time is up last week," said a policeman to a DAILY HERALD representative last night. " I then go on pension, but I can stand big by the others."

Nothing in the world would make me more ashamed of myself than if my mate's wife, or my own child's ask me for bread when I should myself.—George Lansbury.

Marston, who was last night dubbed "The Gold Man," made quick time for West-end last night. He was not there long, he bore he left the Woolwich men were out.

Edmonton Labour Party has conveyed great wishes to the strikers, through Mrs. Webb. She paid a visit to Edmonton Station last night to make sure all would attend the Tower Hill meeting to-day.

The Soldiers', Sailors' and Airmen's Union sent a message to the police last night tendering their sympathy, and declaring their willingness to come out with the strikers if they offered their services as pickets to try and prevent men doing blackleg duty.

IRISH POLICE NEXT?

In answer to a question in Parliament Mr. Macpherson writes : The Inspector-General of the Royal Irish Constabulary, and the officers and constabulary of officers and men, are at present carefully considering the recommendations of Lord Desborough's Committee, and hopes to be able to submit recommendations on the subject at an early date.

CHELSEA FIRST

P.C. Goodman was the first to sign off duty at Chelsea station, and he wishes to point out that, in spite of the allegation that Chelsea had remained loyal to the Commissioner, they are probably the first district in the Metropolis to come out on a man.

KING AND CARDINAL

BRUSSELS, Thursday.—The Libre Belgique states that the King of the Belgians has conferred the insignia of the Order of Leopold on Cardinal Mercier, Archbishop of Malines. Her Vauves Cardinal, King of the Belgians, and Very Rev. Canon Leo, of Clifton Cathedral, have been appointed Chevaliers of the Order de la Couronne for their services to Belgian refugees.—Reuter.

BIG INCREASES IN PENSIONS

Chorus of Applause for Worthington Evans

£96,000,000 A YEAR

By Our Parliamentary Correspondent

WESTMINSTER, Thursday—besides the Minister must with such a chorus of congratulation, on introducing the estimate of pensions, as he did to the lot of Sir L. Worthington Evans this afternoon. The present Minister of Pensions has certainly taken a subject which, as Mr. Hodge, a good judge and a colleague, gave a concrete example of the enormous expanse of the immense cardpost of its Ministry.

The Minister described at some length there that he had introduced in a money a three were no excesses, insufficient disa.. dissolution of arrears ; and are steps in that issues and were taking for obtaining resolution, of the I-state are entirely at an issued unless it is all regulated are an instance of administration and all assist the method and seemed [?be to labour in a attitude working prowess was commendation.

The Statutory Bill

Turning to the reasons, amount support funds constant, that he the million on the man that the amount had to be increased by so and much, owing the of management to the new disabilities, or pensioners, grant of them to acquired so in the..

I with regards to his honorary ministry, each pension with the set up by rate taken to be, doing, amount the date of a permanent, allotted funds cosmic of a single class dissented others or others committee assure me it very cannot up the amount to granted a the estimate would have the available to persons to so, set the amount of pension and allowances.

I was maintained that the conveyor money the the recommended as to work allow the voluntary and it was against to said the revenue any a most importance, at the management therewith.

In the present pensions were already..

Sir Edward Ward as an all to at Royal and the men saying that they shall it's ridiculous to suggest that they will a pension so a problem of to at a said, themselves with any time.

WHAT IT MEANS

The following is a summary of the announced yesterday :—

A single man, 40s., which expresses 12 : a married man, 50s., 17s. rise ; man, with one child, 57s 6d., 13s. with two children, 65s 6d., 15s. 6d. three children, 69s. 6d. 17s. 6d. rise for each subsequent child.

I am aware too too partially due to widows' pensions, the widening take to under the Royal Warrant, or in part means, the flat for widows wife a per cent. the fund to for children and 50s. subsequent child.

In regard to the proposals for of widows' pensions, the retaining rate to those cases where the full is restoring, this rate means, 5s. and per cent. increase on a return, as rising : and the flat to 50 per cent. of a war allowance for soon before wee : man's work, and into the portrait or are unassigned with the flat...

The increased amount of the years : allowances at large over the of the basis of assessment by they sanctioned an employment at a previously increased, and, as that the maximum allowances of up to 50s. a week, or that be taken seventy that the maximum allowance the service would be wherever.

With regard to widows' allowances funds grant present maintaining the at the rate principle of will apply to 40 per cent. for soon after widows, and, notwithstanding the will be fund 60 per cent. of the previous amount.

WOOL KING'S BEQUESTS

MELBOURNE, Thursday.—The estate of the late Sir Samuel M'Caughey has been estimated at £2,000,000. Of this the deceased has bequeathed £500,000 to Sydney University, £250,000 to Brisbane University, £150,000 for the Presbyterian Church, besides making many bequests to colleges and hospitals. Sir Samuel arrived in Australia penniless 60 years ago. For several years now he has been known as the Australian Wool King.—Exchange.

BRITONS FLY TO SPAIN

MADRID, Thursday.—The " Epoca " announces that two British aviators, who left London at 7 o'clock this morning, landed at Madrid at 3 o'clock this afternoon.—Reuter.

APPEAL TO LABOUR

The following appeal is issued to the organised workers of the country by the Executive Committee of the Police Union:—

" The Executive Committee of the National Union of Police and Prison Officers urgently appeals to all sections of organised workers of the country to extend their support which they have from time to time signified their readiness to render, to this Union in its fight against repression.

" We are convinced that, if any Trade Union is permitted to be utterly destroyed by an Act of Parliament, it would be a dangerous precedent and a menace to the whole Trade Union movement.

" We also appeal, as a young Trade Union fighting for the right of existence, to the Trade Union movement to fight for the right of existence, and we feel that the ranks of organised Labour will move to our support in this serious conflict.

(Signed) J. H. HAYES.

(Mr. Marston.)

Union Trumpet

Blown by the *Daily Herald*, but its triumphant note is false. *Daily Herald*.

Blast and Counter-blast

A London wall, where PC strikers show what they think of claims that the strike has failed. *Radio Times Hulton Picture Library.*

The Missing Shields

Riot shield practice for Liverpool policemen, sixty years ahead of the times. *Topical Press.*

Filling the Gap

The blue line gone, there's an SOS for the khaki. The PBI deploy outside St George's Hall. *Liverpool Daily Post and Echo.*

TOP: **Confrontation in London**
Police 'loyalists' make their way through a picket line by the Elephant and Castle

BELOW: **Chaos in Liverpool**
The mob has run amok and a looted clothiers is just one of its early casualties. *Dail*
Mirror.

WE NOW PROTECT OUR BANKS WITH TANKS
POLICE STRIKE

G. 91

TOP: **Replacement on the Beat**
Instead of the man in Blue it takes a tank to guard the bank . . . *Daily Mirror.*

BELOW: **Bayonets Fixed**
Children gawk and pilfer among the ruins. *Daily Mirror.*

The Lawless Streets
Early morning workers see a shopping centre that has changed its face. *Liverpool Daily Post and Echo.*

TOP: **Liverpool Loyalists**
After a night of battle with the mob 'loyalists' of the Flying Column stay on duty in the daylight. *Liverpool Daily Post and Echo.*

BELOW: **The Navy's Here**
Rushed south from Scapa with the battleship Valiant, the destroyer H.M.S. Venomous guards Pierhead. *Daily Herald.*

'A War Zone'
Tanks arrive in Liverpool city centre: 'sledgehammers to crack a nut'. *Daily Mirror*.

The Head Constable begs to submit the following Report on the state of the Force, Absentees, Variations, Rewards, and Punishments, for the Week ended Friday *8th August 1919*

ABSENTEES.

RANK.	No. ABSENT.	NUMBER OF DAYS.				TOTAL DAYS.
		SICK.	HURT.	LEAVE.	ABSENT WITHOUT LEAVE.	
SUPERINTENDENT						
INSPECTOR	1	7				7
SERGEANT	4	13	6			19
CONSTABLE	40	178	27			205
	45	198	33			231

VARIATIONS.

Dismissed ... 955 (Strikers)

Pensioned ...

Resigned ... 4 & 2 Moore

Died ...

Re-joined ... 173 A October 160 A Fairhead 328 A Green 53 F Jones 68 F Goodwin 304 B 128 F 1

Appointed ... 32 Rejoin Pensioners 185 Recruits

Actual Strength 1142

Number required to complete strength ... 1128
2270

PUNISHMENTS.

Dismissed .... Suspended (temporarily) ....

Reduced ....

Fined .... Total Amount of Fines £ ....

REWARDS.

Amount of Watch Committee Rewards - - £ ....

Amount of Private Rewards { - - £ ....

Head Constable.

O.37055. Pbk. 10/16(52705)1145

Stroke of the Pen
955 police strikers are dismissed by the Head Constable of Liverpool.

TOP: **Back on the Beat**
The faces are mostly new. Ex-soldiers to fill the places of the PCs who have lost th
careers. *Daily Mirror.*

BELOW: **Out of the Blue**
Sacked Poplar PCs still contrive to grin, as they use a coster's barrow to return th
uniforms. They share the fate of 1,083 London policemen – not one of whom is e
reinstated. *London Borough of Tower Hamlets Amenities Committee.*

However, with the traditional respect for the virtues of personal leadership appropriate to a top military man, he had also emphasised that no such subterfuge would be resorted to by the more senior ranks. From Sergeants upwards they must be ready at all times to go on to the streets 'to hearten up the men'.

Subversion must be nipped in the bud, wherever it showed itself – defeated by argument, if possible, and – by implication – by brute force if necessary.

Above all, they must re-emphasise that the penalty for joining the strikers would be 'instant dismissal without reinstatement'. There would be no second thoughts on the part of the Government: not on this occasion. There would be no turning back.

As he came to re-examine the directives he had issued to scotch the situation that he had so long anticipated – and may indeed have aimed at – Sir Nevil had every reason to be pleased with the way things were working out.

Enthusiasm for the strike among the early evening and 10 pm shifts had been, with few exceptions, as lukewarm as he had expected. Pickets seeking to bar non-strikers from reporting to their stations had been met by determined opposition.

Several prominent fighters for the Union were now declaring total opposition to the Executive's move, and at Loughton – Marston's own station – not one member of the Union had followed his leader's example. All of them had turned up for duty.

True that the response from certain of the East End districts had been disappointing, while the withdrawal of patrols from other areas – in compliance with the Yard's orders – had deceived more reporters than the *Herald's* into believing Hayes's claims of 'massive support' and, consequently, embarrassingly broadcasting them. But these were but minor annoyances. The situation was being contained.

In A Division, largest in the Metropolis, not a single man had joined the strikers. A similar situation prevailed in C Division, Woolwich and the River Police. In H Division, where militants had claimed to have gained control, it now appeared that only eight PCs had backed their action, the rest had stayed loyal.

As the Strike leaders were already pointing out, it was as yet too early to assess the full response of the force. Many of the men due to parade on subsequent shifts might decide to stay away. Others would not yet have heard of the Executive's decision. And a sizable proportion – maybe a majority – would be seeking clarification of the position before deciding which way to act. But, by and large, the situation appeared to be far more satisfactory than even the optimistic Commissioner had anticipated, and far less menacing than that envisaged by the pessimists, of whom the Yard as well as the Home Office had its quota.

Sir Nevil had additional cause for relief in the reports reaching him from the crime front. To him – and indeed to most of the strikers – a major fear had always been that the criminal elements in the capital would be quick to seize the opportunities for loot and pillage afforded them as the result of a police withdrawal. So far they had been gratifyingly slow.

Trouble might very well arise the following night, but the undesirables had already lost the initiative. By then it should be possible to restore most of the patrols; by Sunday, if his theory should prove correct, it should be possible to return to normal policing.

Sir Nevil, who had left his Assistant Commissioner to return a 'No Comment' answer to Press questions during the early hours of the Strike, now decided that the time had come when it would be prudent, as well as courteous, to indulge the newspapers' natural curiosity.

A statement on the current numbers of the strikers compared with those of the men who had remained loyal would be issued – in time for the early evenings. And, with this, a message with a theme that should be sufficient to convince all who still wavered between the Union and their duty. He would dub it 'this feeble Strike', as an aid to keeping it so.

That, in Liverpool, it would be the very reverse of 'feeble', probably did not occur to this natural publicist as he prepared the latest blow against the militants. But Liverpool, of course, was outside Sir Nevil's sphere . . .

There were those who were to claim that, while Macready had

succeeded in imposing his intensely personal sway upon the Metropolitan Police by getting to know his men and the strength and weaknesses of their grievances, Francis Caldwell, MVO, Head Constable of Liverpool, had been too remote and detached a figure to inspire the force he commanded.

'Never saw him but once – and THAT was when he presented a cup to the Bowling Club,' was Leonard Petchey's assessment when asked about his superior's attributes.

And, in this respect, Petchey had been unusually favoured. Up to the time of the Strike the vast majority of Liverpool's PCs had never seen their Head Constable at all.

On the other hand, to the rare few of the rank and file who, like O'Keeffe, were to have a closer acquaintanceship with the man during the riots that followed in the Police Strike's wake, Caldwell was 'a perfect gentleman, and a brave one too'.

During the worst of the brutal fighting in Scotland Road the Head Constable was to display not only considerable courage but also prove his capacity to lead and understand his men. Unfortunately for his reputation's sake, it was then rather late in the day.

Just short of six feet in height and carrying not an inch of unhealthy fat on his slim and straight-backed frame, Caldwell had the trim and taut stance of the old-time cavalry officer, and could have been mistaken for such: but appearances deceived.

The Head Constable had been a policeman since the start of the nineties, when the Liverpool City Police force was less than sixty years old. In fact, he had been a policeman all his life.

With such a formidable background of experience it might well be wondered – by those with the advantage of hindsight – how it was that he could have so singularly failed to appreciate the gathering resentment of the men, let alone do anything to uncover and resolve the grievances that had fostered it.

An answer to the mystery of this communications gap between Caldwell and his rank and file may have lain in the way he delegated authority: a praiseworthy desire not to 'interfere' with immediate subordinates leading to loss of control at the top.

His Inspectors were said to rule like independent princes. His

Sergeants were described as medieval barons. 'With them in the way,' a PC has since stated, 'it was difficult, if not impossible, for top and bottom of the structure to say as much as Good Morning to each other.'

On the night of 31 July, Francis Caldwell, just short of his sixtieth birthday and his thirtieth year of service, was being called upon to face a crisis that, whether or not he had unknowingly contributed to its cause, was to prove the most dangerous and most complex ever to afflict a British city.

The Head Constable had been advised in the afternoon that the Union leaders in the city were making preparations for a strike, and had decided to spend the night at Police Headquarters in Hatton Garden, conveniently close to the City Hall and commanding the approaches to both Lime Street and Birkenhead.

Like others far less exalted, though for reasons diametrically opposite, Caldwell was anxious for news of the reaction of the night shift and also – perhaps even more needful – the reaction to the Strike in the turbulent community, largely Irish by descent, that crowded the cobbled alleys and back-to-back terraced cottages that sprawled to east and west of Great Homer Street and the Scotland Road, major trouble spots throughout the city's chequered history.

Should the Strike prove effective, he could see a host of ugly consequences arising once the knowledge of it spread among these people; traditionally the underdogs, but all too willing to use their teeth.

Of course, should the Strike prove to be the flop that the Watch Committee's Alderman Maxwell – and Macready, down in London – had been forecasting, then it would be over and done before the mob in Liverpool 8 had a chance to rouse themselves. All the same . . .

Worriedly Caldwell called for an up-to-date report on the situation from the stations that lay in the heart of his troubled empire. And settled down to wait.

The dawn of the first day of August was bright and clear on Merseyside. For Caldwell it had been a long and depressing night: full of disappointment and frustration.

At first, hopes of a quick ending to the Strike had been encouraged by the reports from the individual divisions, showing a comparatively low number of absentees. But these initial returns of strength were followed by others that seemed to make such nonsense of the originals that he had sent them back for a recount.

It was not long, however, before the reason for this disparity became all too painfully clear. Perhaps in an effort to save defaulters from the wrath to come, while they reasoned with them in an attempt to bring them back to duty, certain officers had ventured to cook the books.

Later, word from London – and, in particular, Scotland Yard – had brought slight cheer to the increasingly apprehensive group of senior officers and civic dignitaries who had gathered in the Head Constable's office in the 'Garden': but even this had a bitter anti-climax.

Scarcely had they absorbed Macready's news that, so far, only two hundred and forty men of the Metropolitan Force had followed the Union's lead, and had again begun to hope that this might be the pattern for Liverpool too, than they heard that striking PCs had surrounded the Central Fire Station.

Blowing whistles and shouting slogans, the men had first tried to pull the firemen out in their support and then, this failing, had joined the pickets outside HQ itself. An ominous background to the deliberations of the troubled government of the city, their derisive cheers and chants had lasted until daybreak.

By now it was known that about three hundred members of the force had struck, or approximately a sixth of its total strength.

But, bad though this was, there was bound to be worse to come. Many men who had reported for duty were known to be only postponing their defection. While others, on shift at the time of the Strike's declaration would now have been informed by the Union of the issues at stake, and what was expected of them.

As yet the crisis was only ten hours old, and the bulk of the men would be hesitating, uncertain of their stand. But, once button-holed by the proselytising militants who were now roaming the streets outside the police stations, the Liverpool waverer who plumped for the authorities would be a very rare bird indeed. Old loyalties would be appealed to: in the name of Union solidarity. Old grievances would be recollected, and past comradeship recalled. And, for the recalcitrant, there would be the odious tag of 'Bloody Blackleg'.

But the major fear that dominated Caldwell and those around him was of what the night might bring to the Scotland Road.

It was all very well for the Home Office and the Yard, happy at the way things were shaping in the metropolis, to make encouraging noises over the telephone on the virtues of 'standing firm', but the metropolis had nothing like the frightening range of class, political, religious and racial differences that divided the communities in Liverpool.

In making *his* gamble, Macready had no reason to provide against an eruption of old hatreds from a neighbourhood divided between the Orange and the Green, the Pope and King Billy.

Nor did he have to consider the menace of racial clashes between a small but growing black minority and a dockland resentful of strangers.

And, as a further cause of friction, there was the appalling poverty of the area, and the lawlessness that that poverty had fostered. London, in this respect, was certainly no paradise but, to a sizable proportion of its people, Liverpool more closely resembled hell.

So what happened if, lacking the firm hand that had so often held it down, the lid of this boiling cauldron should blow off and empty its content on the city at large?

The Watch Committee had considered this question too, and had been appalled at the ugliness of the answer. Acting with uncharacteristic celerity they had met in emergency session in response to a plea by the Lord Mayor, but had quickly come to realise the current limitations of their role. They might dictate to the city on what was to be done, but what were words without the force to back them?

Even Alderman Maxwell, beetle-browed, massively built, and as robust as ever in his denunciation of the 'reds and mutineers', seemed to diminish in stature as the meeting debated the options before it. Long used to dominating the Committee scene, even he was beginning to realise that events could impose a domination of their own. Within the limits of the Committee's terms of reference he and his fellow members had imposed their sway by invocation of the law and by use where necessary of its penalties. But the law in turn depended on the men who habitually defended and enforced it. To date, Macready had less than two per cent of his men on strike. In Liverpool that percentage was ten times as great, and there were signs that the underworld was beginning to do its sums . . .

Moodily, reluctantly, but with its anxiety for the city overpowering its resentment at having to swallow its pride, the Committee decided that, whatever London might think, the time had come for Liverpool to reconsider the 'stand firm' policy towards the strikers.

It was decided to circulate all stations and, if possible, each individual policeman with the warning that: 'Every member of the force who does not return to work immediately or parade at his divisional office for orders at 8 pm on this first day of August will be dismissed.'

At first sight there seemed little to distinguish this post-Strike statement from its tough and uncompromising predecessor of 31 March. A second look discovered a significant concession.

Previously it had been stated that 'any member who joins in a strike and fails to perform his ordinary tours of duty will be dismissed'. But now, those who had joined the Strike had been given a second chance, provided they paraded at 8 pm.

It was a shrewd move; one calculated to win back those of the men who, having originally left their beats as a result of intimidation or persuasion by their fellows, had subsequently regretted the move but felt it was too late for them to come back. But it was also a gesture somewhat limited in its effectiveness by the clock – through lack of time the order was never to reach a maximum circulation – and also by the terseness of its wording.

93

A pity, perhaps that the Committee, having bravely decided that, for a good cause, it was willing to risk a considerable loss of face, should have tried, by a form of words, to save what little face remained to it.

PC 'Shiny' Salt was one of the first to hear of the Watch Committee's offer. He had turned up for duty as usual at Wavertree police station, and no striker had attempted to stop him.

Everyone liked and respected 'Shiny' Salt, a bit of a legend in D Division in the embattled Scotland Road before being transferred to this relatively tranquil suburb. Also, they knew there was precious little use in trying to persuade him into anything opposed to either his conscience or his judgment, which currently were in amicable alliance.

'Shiny' had been dead against the Strike idea from the moment it was first mooted. He felt that, whatever their grievances, it was wrong for the police to strike 'and throw the general public to the wolves'. Also he felt that a Strike was doomed to fail.

Remarkable for his slight build and medium height, in a force whose members were type-stamped by their impressive length and breadth, 'Shiny' was also notable for his giant-sized courage: a fighter who would take on the most outrageous odds.

Like Petchey he had been much involved in the riots of Bloody Sunday, and had come under a hail of missiles when marching with the men of his old division from Rose Hill to Lime Street. He had been one of the foremost in the repeated police charges that had followed the attack, and had taken the consequences with fortitude and aplomb. Even when a broken bottle had been gouged into his knee, Shiny had continued with the fight.

He had also been in the thick of the more recent sectarian riots, when an Orange parade had been ambushed by adherents of the Green, and its drum-major, badly injured, was subsequently attacked by the boot brigade, when lying in the gutter.

Acting with his customary pluck, Salt had intervened to protect the man, and in turn had become the target of the mob. Blows and kicks had fallen on him from all directions, but he had never retreated an inch. When comrades came to the rescue, and packed him off for medical care, they could not make up their minds as to what had damaged him the most, a length of lead piping or a jagged brick.

But, temporarily at least, Salt's fighting days were over. The police authorities had decided he had had enough. They had posted him to G Division, offering pleasant surroundings for his family, and fixed him up with an inside job, as Station Keeper.

Which is why he was one of the first to hear of 'the eight pm extension'.

'General clerk and general dogsbody' as he described his role, Shiny Salt got the word when he answered a telephone call from Hatton Garden. It came to him as a great relief, a chance of survival in the force for old mates who otherwise would have been barred from it for ever.

Already it was apparent that the Strike was failing in London, and he was convinced that this would mean its failure in Liverpool too. To succeed, the Union's action had to be national, or nothing. The city force had been led out on a limb.

Well, here was a chance at least to get them down before it broke. 'I'll take the word round to their homes myself,' he volunteered. 'Just to make sure they get it.'

'Some of the diehards may give you a pretty rough reception,' the Inspector said, a little dubious.

'But a lot will be glad to get back, I'm sure of that Sir,' Salt replied. 'And there won't be any hard feelings, even among those who won't.'

In Liverpool it was a tradition of the Station Keeper's job that its incumbent did not wear uniform, and for this – on the current occasion – Shiny was duly grateful. Unburdened by anything heavier than his summer civvies, he would be able to move faster, and thus cover more ground.

There were a lot of names on the list he carried in his breast pocket. Eight o'clock was not an eternity away.

The situation was becoming increasingly explosive. A local businessman has since affirmed that, as he stared from his office window at the busy crowds who thronged the street below, he could sense in this appearance of the everyday the electrically-charged calm that precedes a tropical storm. He could feel the tension settling over the city as positively as if it was a physical experience.

As the afternoon wore on, a similarly sombre exercise in imagination was preoccupying the group of anxious civic dignitaries who had mustered around Caldwell in Hatton Garden. His Worship the Lord Mayor, Alderman John Ritchie was among them.

Ritchie had a military background, and the rank of Lieutenant-Colonel, but this current conflict was something quite outside his experience. When they first told him that the trusted City Police had 'mutinied' he had described the news as 'incredible'. He still found it next to incredible even now.

'Mr Ritchie was intensely proud of his city, but it's likely that he thought of it in terms of its splendid showpieces – St George's Hall, the Walker Gallery, the Liver Building and places like that,' a former police officer has recorded. 'And, of course, he was also proud of the trade and enterprise that had made those showpieces possible.

'To him, we PCs must have been just part of this image of prosperity and success . . . the man in blue . . . sound fellows all. Whether holding the crowds back at some glittering civic function, or plunging into the Mersey to save somebody from drowning, or merely warning a school kid to be more careful when crossing the road, you could always rely on the police force. It was always around when needed.

'Looking at things that way, it must have been a tremendous shock to him when the men in whom so much confidence had been placed walked off the beat. A great patriot, he even believed those who dubbed the strikers as "bolsheviks". He really did not know what it was all about.'

The police officer concluded: 'I don't think he had even the foggiest idea of the meanness with which those who ran the city treated its so-called "indispensable" police service.'

The situation, as presented to the Lord Mayor on his arrival at the Garden, in military terms would have been classed as 'fluid'.

Apart from a few sporadic clashes between strikers and 'loyalists' where surprisingly – considering their formidable reputation – neither party had seemed to do the other very much damage, the progress of the strike so far had been relatively undramatic.

News had come in from the Birkenhead force across the river. The local branch of the Union had put the issue to the vote, but had failed to get the necessary one-third majority. The Wallasey men were also remaining loyal, but in Bootle the situation was still obscure.

A strong group of Liverpool strikers had assembled to march on the town and call on these near-neighbours to join them. They were now on their way, blowing whistles as they went.

This latter move was certainly no storming of the Winter Palace, but it was sufficient to still further dismay the city bigwigs. That the Liverpool men should have done the inconceivable and bitten the hand that fed them, so to speak, was bad enough; for them to act as rabble rousers, inciting their colleagues in other areas to join the 'mutiny' was a shameful thing for the reputation of the city: the reputation of the city fathers too.

For Ritchie, however, there had to be broader considerations than the strikers' challenge to authority's *amour propre*. Like Caldwell, his major concern was what the strike might mean to the community at large, the community of which he was still the titular head.

There was still some time to run before 8 pm and the expiry of the 'amnesty' (though no member of the Watch Committee would have dared to call it this) and still hope that, before that time was reached, at least some of the errant sheep would have returned to the fold. Meanwhile, however, the scene was scarcely conducive to optimism.

When even the city's massive Police HQ was forced to rely on a handful of volunteers and rookies for garrison, resources would be sparse indeed for the back streets of Liverpool 8.

Increasingly mindful of the danger ahead but unable, by the

nature of things, to address the strikers direct and plead with them to return, Ritchie now decided to do the next best thing: address the loyalists and appeal to them to stand firm.

'The men will be glad to hear from you,' said Caldwell. 'It will be good for their morale.'

Ritchie hoped he was right.

CHAPTER SEVEN

His Worship Takes the Chair

'I've seen some strange sights in Flanders,' reflected Gerald O'Keeffe, 'but nothing stranger than this.'

When Harrison and he, still bewildered by their encounter with the Sergeant from Seel Street, arrived in Hatton Garden's austere parade-room it had been so full of PCs that, at first sight, they had thought all that 'Police Strike' talk had been an elaborate legpull. Someone had been trading on their innocence.

But the PCs, it became evident, were newcomers like themselves, recruits in training. With the exception of the station Sergeant and two or three other trusties, not one of the usual veterans was to be seen. And then, as they joined the men discussing this phenomenon and tried to glean from the morning papers what the crisis was about, an Inspector had appeared, and called them to attention.

The situation, he said crisply, was one of 'mutiny'. It was an insult to all that the force had come to stand for, and would be put down. But after he had read out the Watch Committee's warning and concluded his brief version of events with a resounding declaration of his confidence in their loyalty and discipline, O'Keeffe was still in a haze as to what was the cause of it all. In fact, his main impression was one of wonderment at the way in which the Inspector had addressed them as 'My Lads'.

Such an attempt at 'chumminess' by a superior towards PCs was so rare in the Liverpool force that the squad found it almost embarrassing. The situation must be serious indeed.

And now, to crown this morning of extraordinary events, they had before them the spectacle of a worried-looking man, with a gold chain around his shoulders, climbing cautiously on to a rickety chair so as better to be seen by them all and introducing himself as the Lord Mayor, come in person to speak to them.

'A full Lieutenant-Colonel, or used to be,' whispered Harrison, 'but looks a wee bit peaky don't you think?'

O'Keeffe impatiently hushed him, and tried to concentrate on what His Worship was saying.

It was a speech that was unprepared, and lacked completely the felicitous tone of phrase employed in the observance of more routine occasions: but probably it was none the worse for that.

As Ritchie, nervously clearing his throat between each sentence, launched his stumbling and anxious appeal for loyalty during 'this incredible crisis', the first of its kind in the force's 83 years of service, the gravity of the occasion began to dawn on his audience. And with this came a grudging sympathy for the man. City bigwig or not, his was more than a pep talk: he was baring his soul.

'The whole community relies upon your loyalty and sense of duty,' he continued. 'The security of the city depends on you.'

Coming from someone who had so often presided in the council chamber with an authority of almost frightening power, O'Keeffe found the statement 'somewhat incongruous'. For those with personal experience of the way their 'loyalty and sense of duty' had been regarded by the city in the past, the simile would have seemed an understatement. The thoughts of the newcomers, however, were confined strictly to the present. When the Lord Mayor came down from his perch he was rewarded by applause.

Following Ritchie's departure from the room, the recruits again found themselves with time on their hands. Training sessions had been cancelled 'for the next few days' but they were to remain available for further orders. On no account were they to leave the building.

Harrison said: 'So it's CB then?'

'You'll wait your orders,' the Inspector answered.

But for once there was no frantic desire among the squad to break out of the Garden's gloom and go for the pub on the corner. They were too intrigued by the mystery of the events around them: each putting forward his own theory of what would be expected of them next.

'They're bound to call in the army,' said O'Keeffe. 'It stands to reason. If there's no more than us lot left to cope with the trouble ahead, then Heaven help the city.'

Hardly had he got the words out than a voice remarked, with unpleasant emphasis, 'Forget about the city. You worry about US!'

The speaker stood in the doorway of the parade-room, a broad-shouldered, aggressive looking fellow in civilian clothes.

'What the hell do *you* think you're doing here?' a young PC pompously challenged. 'This room is for police use only; not for the general public.'

'I was here when you were in nappies, son,' the man replied. He swayed slightly, and they caught the tang of stale spirit. 'They're leading you up the garden path, I tell you. Turning you into a pack of bleeding blacklegs.'

Another man in civilians stepped through the door, hand raised placatingly to restrain the argument. 'He's put it badly, brothers, but in a way he's right. Your place is out there, with your comrades.' This time the hand pointed to the street.

Like the eager Sergeant from Seel Street, the newcomers were Union militants, anxious to emphasise the need for solidarity, and pressing them to enrol as NUPPO members. But the recruits were confused in their feelings, and still influenced by Ritchie's appeal.

The men had a good case, doubtless, but it was too late in the day to sell it to the recruits now. Ex-soldier O'Keeffe, for one, had flinched at the Inspector's use of the word 'mutiny' to describe the Union's action. The Jerries might mutiny, and the French and Russians too: but never a Briton.

Nor was the 'Strike' tag much more satisfactory. Strikes were all right for civilians – munitions workers and the like – but they were not for men in uniform. Men in uniform knew their duty.

'It's no use,' he found himself saying. 'For better or worse we've taken the Oath, and that's all to it.'

'Nobody gets dismissed if he's back on the job by 8 pm,' said

101

Harrison, seconding him. 'So why not call it a day. You've put the wind up the Mayor, and the top brass too – they're bound to meet you, if you start to offer terms.'

It was no go. The London men were 'out' the sober one explained and for Liverpool men to back down at such a time would be a complete betrayal. But the discussion would probably have continued if it had not been for his companion. 'Cowards and traitors,' he suddenly yelled at them. 'You're frightened of your own shadows.'

Cowards and traitors! And most of them just back from the hell of the Western Front.

'You'll say you're sorry for that,' said someone, breaking the ugly pause; but he only yelled the louder, and suddenly tempers snapped. They grabbed the man and rushed him across the parade-room, then hustled him down the steps into the street.

'The only argument a Liverpool man understands is a clout. And a few clouts handed out at the beginning would have saved a lot of trouble.'

This unflattering view of the Liverpool community appeared in a Manchester newspaper at the height of the mob violence and ostensibly was that of 'a PC from Bury'. It says much for the mood of the time that, far from rushing to the defence of its readers, the *Liverpool Echo* not only reprinted the PC's comments but also gave them the support of a leading article, in which it stated:

The constable does not understand psychology but he has weighed the Liverpool man in the balance and found out what he lacks. He was absolutely right. We have heard the expression 'a Manchester man and a Liverpool gentleman', but it is an unfortunate fact that there is a larger proportion of toughs in Liverpool than in any other British city. The civic history of the city is a record of sporadic ebullitions of mob violence. Anyone who knows the Scotland Road area understands its latent possibilities of riot and plunder whenever the chance is given.

To PC Tom O'Brien, of Liverpool's A Division, the *Echo*'s leader came as no revelation. It contained nothing new. It was merely a statement of fact. Nor would he have found much to quarrel with in his Bury colleague's prescription for the health of Scotland Road: Tom had handed out 'good clouts' himself when forced to cope with certain of its residents. Yet, as one who had spent quite a bit of his working life on this most unsalubrious of beats, he would also have argued that its vices were the result more of the course of history than an excess of original sin.

'The city grew up too fast,' he used to say. 'In forcing the plant they overdid the manure.'

In less than a century, Liverpool had developed from little more than a fishing village into one of the world's great cities and Britain's second busiest seaport. It boasted civic and commercial buildings of grandiose style and quality, and the Liver birds looked down upon a Merseyside that covered over thirty-three square miles of hill and plain, and absorbed into its midst 800,000 people. But, if its opulence was manifest, so too, were its miseries: result of a population explosion unprecedented in any other part of the country.

They had built the first docks in 1805 when Nelson was fighting Trafalgar. In the next thirty years they had added seven more, and imported a horde of unskilled labourers to man them.

By 1846 these, and their progeny, had totalled 240,000 with whole families settling in single rooms and cellars.

Each time he went on patrol O'Brien was confronted by the legacy of those decades: scores of slum tenements, mile upon mile of back-to-back cottages, earth closets that stank in summer and bred a host of flies . . . the place might have been a vast museum piece, devoted to the industrial revolution, or an illustration of the shadow cast by 'black satanic mills'.

But if Liverpool 5 had not changed much in appearance over the years, neither had the outlook of a big proportion of its people. The bitterness and insecurity left over from the time when jobs were on a casual basis and a foreman's frown could mean empty bellies for the wife and kids, had roots that were deep and sick.

Macready, contemplating with some degree of satisfaction the contrast between the behaviour of the Metropolitan Police Force with that of Liverpool during the Strike period, was to put the blame for the latter's troubles on its 'large numbers of Irishmen'.

Tom O'Brien would have been interested in this view, particularly as – erroneously – Macready himself had often been described in the press as being of Irish extraction. Practically a kinsman, so to speak.

The Irish had followed the Welsh into the over-crowded city. They had come in their tens of thousands fleeing the potato famine. Crossing the St George's Channel in ships that used them as ballast – at 2/6d [12½p] a head – they had settled along the Merseyside because it was the first refuge they reached, and they were too exhausted, too impoverished to push on.

By the end of the first year there were 300,000 of them, with typhus and other diseases following in their wake. The primitive sewerage system soon broke down. The medical services were overwhelmed. The dead were buried in mass graves, while famine reduced the living to skeletons, fighting each other for scraps.

And, as the death statistics soared, so also did the crime rate. The police were broken by the sheer weight of numbers against them. And, as the rest of the community starved, the criminals grew fat.

Only when it learned that 20,000 special constables had been sworn in, and that several thousand regular troops were being brought into the city to save it from total anarchy, did Westminster respond to the pleas of the civic authorities to restrain the 'invasion', and reverse its flow.

A special Act of Parliament was rushed through both Houses giving the local authorities power to return destitute immigrants to Ireland; but this drastic move still permitted a sizable proportion of the newcomers to stay behind, and this they did; O'Brien's ancestors were among them.

'People like me,' he used to joke, 'are part of Ireland's atonement. We're forced to live and suffer here, just to make the place respectable.' Always good for a laugh was Tom O'Brien.

Yet though it would have taken more than the combined resources of the O'Brien ilk and their English and Scots colleagues in every police force in the country to have made the Scotland Road 'respectable', at least the Liverpool City men had done a lot to make it safer.

Merseyside was rich indeed in local villains, largely preying on the mass of the local working folk. Heavy-handedly, the force had prevented their excesses from getting worse. The area's 'latent possibilities of riot and plunder', to quote the *Echo*, were all too plain to see, but so far the police had succeeded in ensuring that those traits stayed 'possibilities', and did not become ungovernable. Was tonight to prove an exception?

Tom O'Brien had first heard that the Strike was 'on' when, on his way to the station, he had been stopped by an excited colleague in the street. For Tom, no firebrand, the Union's action seemed premature. He felt, he said, that they had played their trump too soon. He had Norah, his wife, and their three small kids to keep: the Desborough pay recommendations should enable him to do this. He was convinced all the same, that this Government bounty might never have arrived if it had not been for the Union's initial show of muscle. So perhaps now was the time to say thank you, as a paid-up Union member.

Tom O'Brien had more than earned his stipend. The city fathers and the city's millionaires had received their insurance policy at a cut-price rate, he felt. He owed them nothing. And, although he had done his stint with Petchey and Silk during the worst of the confrontations between organised labour and the police, he failed to draw the same conclusions from them.

It was possible, he was convinced, for both sides to work together. Their hostility was skin-deep and very far from permanent. 'We all want fair do's,' he had recently argued. 'We've got a lot more in common than any of us care to own.'

And now, it would appear, this view was proving justified. 'It's all in the *Herald*, Tom,' the excited striker had told him. 'They're lining up the unions behind us!'

Railwaymen, miners and dockers: to judge by the pledges of

their elected members, the thesis advanced by O'Brien – and socialist Tom Milburn – had been correct from the start. Len Petchey had said 'it's all a lot of hot air' when referring to the speeches in the Stadium, but now it was evident that Petchey had been wrong.

The Police Strike was on and the workers would support it. So what was PC Tom O'Brien to do?

He still held that the choice of time was wrong. Better for the Union to have gone underground – as before 1918 – than to have forced a showdown at this particular point, where its action was bound to be represented as a challenge to the will of Parliament. Better for the Union to have kept its powder dry, against the time when the Government could be seen to be the aggressor.

It was not an entirely original line of reasoning: O'Brien was no Liverpool Machiavelli. In fact, quite a few Union notables had advanced it but, as was now apparent, to very little avail.

The theory was that, once the Government – confronted by the 'banned' NUPPO's refusal to die quietly – invoked the Act and sacked Union members from the service, public sympathy would swing heavily to the side of those 'victimised'. The authorities would be cast in the role of heartless oppressors, and the Strike card could then have been played on an easily understandable issue.

It was a pity, Tom felt, that this plan should have been turned down. Had it gone through, it would have eased so many consciences, his own, for one. For then it would have been the Government's fault and not the Union's should the Strike have led to unpleasant repercussions in the streets. Here, on the Scotland Road, such repercussions were already beginning to be felt.

At this stage the local reaction was relatively mild, with a few 'shawlies' – mothers and their urchins – giving ironic and obscene vocal encouragement to a group of men on picket, engaged in arguments with colleagues on their way to work.

But O'Brien knew that later things would begin to get a lot rougher. The women and kids had been sent ahead to test the climate, and see how far it was safe to pit the police against each other.

106

Only when they found there were none of the heavy clouts with palm or cape that normally would have rewarded such impertinence would the district's choicest villains emerge from their lurking-places, and then God help all those who got in their way.

Like so many others who had received the Strike call, O'Brien was initially undecided as to what his response should be. What a Strike would mean to Norah and the kids was a daunting prospect, in fact quite frightening: the O'Briens had seen the face of hunger in their time. Daunting, too, was the thought of what a strike could mean to the community at large: and particularly those in the hinterland of deprived Liverpool 5.

Only when it was put to him by one of the strikers that to refuse would mean abandoning those of his colleagues who already 'taken the jump' did he decide that those early scruples should be set aside.

'If it's not made clear that we're all in this together,' the striker said, 'then God knows what they'll do to the early men.'

And then the argument was also advanced of the effect a low walkout would have on the other unions. Already their leaders had pledged their support for the police action. It would be disgraceful should the police fail to respond. The other unions had rallied to the call of the Police Union. How could that Union's members let their own leaders down?

Tom O'Brien pushed all reservations to the background. He had reached his decision, and would abide by it. London was 'out'. His own mates were 'out'. So must he go 'out' as well. Grimly, he turned off from his beat, and started rather self-consciously on the long walk home.

As he did so, a frightened-looking little man emerged from the doorway of a nearby shop and, after a furtive look at the gathering crowd, began to put up the shutters.

A few minutes later his neighbour of the shop next door started to put up HIS window shutters too, then firmly place a padlock on the door.

Reflecting that he need not put a pint upon the windowsill, his 'acknowledgements' to the copper on the beat – for tonight there would be no copper on the beat – the Irish landlord of the boozer in the side street, wishing a hearty curse upon all strikers, decided to pour himself a stiff one before dispatching the lad to recruit a couple of extra bouncers. They were likely to be needed, in the bloody, black night to come.

Down in London, they had their problems too, even though as Macready had contemptuously put it, the Strike had been a 'fiasco' from the start.

As the early morning shift reported for duty at Old Street they were met by a solid line of pickets, composed not only of strikers but also volunteer supporters from other unions. Tempers flared, fighting broke out, and before reinforcements arrived to restore order four 'loyalist' PCs had been so badly injured that they landed in hospital.

Another group of strikers had marched on the police sector house at Islington and, predictably refused admission, had taken the refusal as excuse for rushing the place and breaking into the hallway. There, however, they were counter-attacked by the very men they had hoped to convert and hurled very much the worse for wear into the street.

Yet although both incidents had ended in 'victory' for Macready's policy – his exhortations to officers and men to 'defend themselves by all means' had obviously been taken to heart – their implications caused considerable concern at both the Home Office and the Yard. A 'civil war' in the ranks of the Metropolitan police was the last thing to be desired: but should the violence and bitterness between the parties evidenced in these two affrays be a true guide to the situation in other divisions this was just what they were going to get.

Only Macready remained unmoved by it all. Although, by 6 am the total of police officers refusing duty had risen to 965, or over double the figure reported three hours earlier, Sir Nevil refused to be ruffled. The number of those who had struck was far below that forecast by even the most optimistic of the intelligence surveys he had commissioned before the Strike began. And the spirit of the non-strikers had shown itself to be far more spirited and aggressive than that of the year before. Sir Nevil faced the future with confidence: it was now the Strike leaders' turn to be racked by doubt.

The Union had called for a mass rally at Tower Hill, but expectations that this would equal the massive demonstration of 1918 were quickly disappointed. The crowd totalled slightly less than a thousand, and it was estimated that less than a third of those present were policemen: and not all of them were sympathisers.

In fact, thanks to the Commissioner's policy of keeping his 'loyalists' off the beat and confined to their stations, the Strike leadership had only the patchiest idea of the extent of the response to its call, and the rally – planned as a demonstration of unity that would carry the waverers into the ranks of the militants – served more to depress than to exhilarate. Its small attendance an indication of the limitations of the Strike's appeal.

Bravely, Marston and Hayes attempted to make the best of things: the former even raising the spirits of the audience by a speech in which, pouring scorn on Lloyd George's refusal to meet the delegates, he declared to loud applause, 'this time the Prime Minister will have to come and see me'.

But, this apparent confidence notwithstanding, there were those who saw a strong element of unease in the anger he displayed when referring to those who had not 'come out'.

A list was being prepared of their names and stations, he said 'so that the executive can take the appropriate action against those who are not men enough to fight for freedom.'

Looking back on the happenings of the day, one of the men who was present at the rally has since told the author 'somehow I felt my heart sinking as I heard Jim hold forth like that. It was then that I first realised the turnout couldn't have been all that we'd been promised it would be. Even Tommy Thiel's fiery speech-making couldn't make me feel any better after that. . . .'

In fact the only crumb of cheer was a telegram from the Liverpool force that claimed – quite erroneously – that the city was out 'solid' and had won over the fire service.

Presiding over the rally was eloquent Jack Zollner. A sergeant in the City of London Police Force but also one of the Union's most fanatical militants. Zollner had backed his principles by being the first – and only – man to walk out on the night shift. Soon he was being pressed by one of his hearers on what had gone wrong with the rest of the force's Union members. Had he not promised that the City would come out to a man?

'Just wait until tonight,' he snapped back. 'You'll get your answer then.'

Zollner had argued from the start that the Strike notice had been too short: there would not be enough time in which to prepare the members. He had also pointed out that the Strike date took no account of the fact that Friday was pay day in the City force, and that on this particular Friday, the back pay of £10 that had been recommended by the Desborough Committee was also due for distribution.

It was unlikely therefore, that anyone on the night or early shift would choose to walk out immediately and thus forfeit the cash. The next night, however, they would have had their brass, and the situation could be very different.

Despite such attempts at reassurance, the Tower Hill crowd dispersed in an unusually thoughtful mood.

'Just wait until tonight . . .' Marston, tackled by the Press not only echoed Zollner's words but, even more explicitly named the very hour that he expected the City Police to rally to the Union. 'Just wait until ten o'clock . . .' he said.

Eager for his colleagues to prove themselves, and justify his earlier promises, Zollner had called an evening conference of kindred souls to pull out the City Force in bulk.

Meeting in an improvised HQ in a gloomy Victorian lecture hall attached to St Botolph's Church, they consisted of representatives of other unions as well as NUPPO members, and by nine o'clock their plans were complete.

They would march to Bishopsgate and meet the men of the ten o'clock shift as they came out of the police station. Free as they then would be of the surveillance of the Inspectors and

Sergeants, the latter would surely join them, and the combined groups could then proceed to picket the remaining 'City' stations.

Such was the theory, but it was emphasised that the action must be pressed home with the utmost energy. If sweet words of persuasion did not work, then threats must be resorted to: Zollner was determined to get a big response.

Almost from the start of the exercise, things were depressingly different from the pattern the Committee had so confidently prepared.

As the strikers, about thirty strong, assembled outside the station a crowd – scenting excitement – began to gather in their rear, and the Committee began to fret that the shift might be detained inside the building until the scene looked less well publicised. They need not have worried.

The clock in the church tower had just finished striking the hour when the first of the Bishopsgate Constables came into the street, and was immediately accosted by the eager pickets. But then things began to go seriously wrong.

Instead of halting to listen to his would-be persuaders, the PC angrily thrust them aside. He did not hold with the bloody Strike, he exclaimed. It had been done in his name, yet he had never been consulted. And who the hell did Zollner think he was, anyway? He was going straight home, and no-one was going to stop him. As he boarded his bus, a few scattered boos accompanied him, but in general the reaction was one more expressive of disappointment than of rage.

The next members of the shift to leave the station came in a group, bunched together, and moved towards the picket line as if tensed to tackle a mob.

'They're looking for bother,' said someone, flexing his muscles. For a moment hostilities waited on one cross word as the men, passing through the pickets, followed their colleagues' example and made for the bus stop.

The strikers' one and only recruit was one of the last PCs to leave the building. When he said he would never again report for duty until the battle was won, he was met by a mighty cheer, and

111

half a dozen of the pickets shook him warmly by the hand. It was as if he was a regiment, instead of one lone young man.

A moment later, the Union men were cheering again, but this time their cheers were ironic. A detachment of mounted police had come cantering along the street, dispersing the bystanders and coming to a halt only a few feet in front of the picket line and the mass of the crowd behind it.

By now this had trebled in numbers, and was several hundreds strong. People who had run from their homes and pubs to 'see the fun', they were in holiday mood and had blocked the roadway, bringing the traffic to a stop.

Nudging his horse forward, the officer in charge of the Mounties tried to make himself heard, and restore the scene to order.

'You are required to move back, please, and keep out of the road. Everyone get back, and on to the pavements.'

He was answered not only by the derisive shouts of the strikers and their supporters but also by a cacophony of motor horns, and applause – and counter-applause – from passengers on the tops of the halted buses.

Stiff-backed as a statue in his saddle, he tried again, had his words drowned by the din and then, as he raised his gloved hand, the line of horsemen advanced.

It was when a group of the police strikers tried to stage a rush that the fighting began but it was half-hearted in character, and very quickly over.

Riding over the pavements, and supported by a strong force of foot police, breaking the crowd into half a dozen segments, the mounted detachment obtained their objective. Within minutes the picket line had been forced back to some distance from the station, and there followed an uneasy truce.

Disappointedly, the spectators began to disperse and return to their homes. At 11.15 a reporter from the *Daily Mirror* asked one of the strikers what happened next, and got the answer: 'I've been up for two days and a night, and intend to stick it out. We're going to see which has the stronger legs: us, or the horses.'

Yet, despite their disappointment at their lack of impact on the outgoing shift, the pickets' vigil had not been altogether fruitless. Some of the men of the new shift, on their way to the station, had been induced to stay away and others, hearing reports of the trouble in Bishopsgate, had not even bothered to start their journey.

By the small hours of Saturday, the Strike's tally in the City of London totalled fifty. It was to rise to fifty-eight but unfortunately, from Zollner's point of view, was not to exceed that figure. Already the predominant feeling in the City Police Force was that the Strike as a whole was becoming a major flop: few men could be expected to stake their future, and that of their families on a gesture only. Sir William Nott-Bower was able to inform his opposite number in the 'Met' that all was quiet.

Quiet on the crime front also was reported from the City wards, though this happy state did not always apply beyond them. On the far side of the river, local villains were just beginning to wake up. Ted Smith was one who witnessed the results of their awakening.

When Ted saw what they'd done to Mrs Hecht's jewellery shop, the *Daily Mirror*'s description of those concerned as 'callous ruffians' was ladylike compared with what he said.

They had forced open the shutters, smashed the plate-glass window and removed practically everything, even down to watch glasses.

'And she a widow, with a child to support!' a neighbour exclaimed with anger. 'Time for the law to gèt back to work again, and do its job in protecting decent people . . .'

There had long been a love-hate relationship between the police and those who lived and worked around the Old Kent Road. At first news of the Strike, circulating by bush telegraph way ahead of the morning papers, the love side predominated.

When a pair of strikers were spotted in East Street market the stallholders loudly cheered them, and an off-duty PC who hitherto had been notoriously unpopular – a scourge of street bookmakers – was plied with pints and enthusiastically advised by his former clients: 'You stand up for your rights, mate, we're all of us on your side.'

It had not always been like that. They had long prided themselves in Bermondsey on being good neighbours – the poor had to help the poor – and never was this more evident than when the law had launched its periodic, and usually abortive, swoops on the local betting industry, in which Ted Smith, at eighteen, was serving a promising apprenticeship.

Soon as he saw the advancing helmet tops loom over the heads of the shoppers Ted would knock at the nearest door, run through the hall to the backyard, then nip over the wall into the house next door: sometimes even re-emerging in time to stand in the crowd behind the police, still trying to get access to his original bolthole. Never once had a door been shut to him, and never once had he failed to send a 'thank-you' to the occupier. The Old Bill, as the police were known, had been beaten once again.

There had, of course, been occasions when the law had the last laugh, such as when one of those warm-hearted neighbours had been tending a stray dog. It had turned on the tresspasser, ripped the seat out of his trousers, pursued him and finally tripped him up. The PC who had collared him had almost died of laughing.

Yet there were few hard feelings on either side in those intermittent forays, which were part of a game rather than a confrontation. Not even the devotees of the Crown and Anchor schools, much though they resented interruption, could get unduly worked up about the police intrusion on their democratic liberties. Besides, thanks to NUPPO's agitation in the Press, they now knew how small was the stipend on which the coppers had had to live. Less than half the wages of a labourer in the docks.

With all this in mind, Ted's first reaction to the idea of a Police Strike was less one of liberation than of grudging sympathy: 'I felt sorry for the coppers. Why shouldn't they have their union?' But he was also, he confesses, extremely tickled by it all. The Law against the Law, it was bound to be comical. Just who nicked who, if both sides came to a punch-up?

In the small hours of the morning, however, the 'comedy' had worn pretty thin, and the Old Kent Road's reputation for good neighbourliness had taken a nasty knock.

From what Ted Smith could make of it, no less than three

separate gangs of looters had taken part in the stripping of widow Hecht's shop. After the first group, who had done the breaking, had left the scene, well-laden with their swag, a second had gone in to help themselves to the bulk of what remained. A third had struck a little later, and had shown its lack of any apprehension of interruption in its work by boldly putting all the lights on.

Nor had Mrs Hecht been the only sufferer in the area. Other looters had forced their way into a greengrocer's, a tobacconist, a draper's and two smaller shops. Nearby, Tower Bridge Road had also had a thorough 'going-over', from a gang who, after raiding another shop, had forced open the doors of the Thrasher Manufacturing Company in Green Walk and escaped with several rolls of cloth and scores of raincoats.

'They then came back, in a stolen car,' a frightened eyewitness said, 'and pinched a lot more.'

'But didn't anyone have a go at stopping them?' Ted enquired.

'Against a crowd like that – armed with axes and jemmies? You must be bloody well joking!'

'Be fair, it's a police job, mate,' another man interrupted. 'That's what we pay them for . . .'

Time indeed for the law to get to work again.

CHAPTER EIGHT

Of Clouts Galore

In Liverpool's Tue-brook district visible signs of the crisis that had hit the city's police force were almost non-existent. While the tension rose – and the shop shutters did too – in the central and dockland areas, the suburb was relaxing, in preparation for the weekend.

On his way to the police station, to report for the night shift, PC Leonard Petchey reflected that he had seldom seen a more tranquil summer's evening: with luck his patrol should be no more than a leisurely stroll.

It was only when he entered the tiny parade-room, and saw the Inspector there – his appearance unwontedly flustered – that he realised that others might have different plans for him.

Petchey and the other seven Constables on the shift were to remain inside the station and 'on call', the Inspector said to assist, if required, their colleagues in less fortunate areas, which seemed to make sense. But then followed an appeal to their sense of loyalty and Len Petchey, hating dramatics, thought irritably, 'The man's all nerves. He's got the wind up.'

All the same, to judge by the latest news, the situation was undoubtedly worsening. The strikers' march on Bootle had been successful, with practically all of the Bootle force coming out to join them. And Birkenhead, which earlier had rejected the Strike call, was said to be having second thoughts. Over two hundred Liverpool men had crossed the Mersey to induce this change of mind, and fighting had broken out between them and a handful of local loyalists.

'They'll be coming for us next,' said one of the PCs.

'If they do, we'll give them a bloody rude answer,' Petchey

replied, still peeved at the drama that had interrupted his tidy routine.

The telephone rang, and the inspector jumped at the sound. Grabbing the instrument, he waved them to silence, and then, after a few terse words, replaced the receiver and said:

'They're on their way. A crowd of strikers and their hangers-on.'

'So what do we do, sir? Defend the station?'

He had scarcely got the words out when they heard the whistles and the chanting. The threatened procession was almost in sight.

The Inspector considered the situation, and then said: 'We don't want trouble, if it can be avoided. We'll get out!'

They could hardly believe their ears.

'We'll leave the station by the back door, and go over the back wall,' the officer added. 'We don't want any unnecessary heroics . . .'

Heroics! Petchey had no wish for a brawl with former colleagues, but this, he felt, was about 'the giddy limit'.

Last man to leave, he made his exit in great embarrassment, his feelings made none the easier by the realisation that a group of small boys had gathered, to get the most of the spectacle.

'What are those men doing climbing the wall?' one of them asked.

'They're running away from the police,' the other answered.

Heroics be damned!

In the Garden they would not have thought very highly of the Tue-brook's reluctance to get involved: blood and guts pep talks were the order of the day.

So extreme was the terminology employed that there were times when O'Keeffe felt he was back in the trenches, being steeled to attack at dawn.

The tactics discussed were equally familiar and, on the whole, the recruits' school was glad of it. Police Law, traffic control, the rights of the individual and the power of arrest . . . the curriculum they had found such heavy going had vanished at the first

117

hint of trouble boiling up in the city's slums. Academic dissertations had given place to plans for physical action.

Caldwell, no longer aloof and undecided, had decreed that first priority must be given to preventing – or at least containing – any widespread eruption of the traditional turbulence of the Scotland Road community, by now fully aware of the division within the force and no doubt already sizing up the prospects it offered them of easy profit at only nominal risk.

At first, Caldwell had tried a bluff: sending out every 'regular' he could still command to the trouble centres to convey an illusion of normality. But the bluff had been called, and indeed had even misfired, with the 'locals' as yet merely curious and probing – noting the absence of so many familiar faces. And many of the men, operating individually or in small detachments, had succumbed to the persuasion of the highly mobile pickets.

Faced with this dilemma, the Chief Constable took a fresh look at the position of the recruits whom, hitherto, he had planned to employ in a purely defensive role, manning the stations.

They knew nothing about the techniques of crowd control and would be next to useless for 'normal' policing, but the night ahead would be very far from 'normal', and these were willing lads with plenty of hard muscle.

It was in the early afternoon that the Head Constable, revising earlier plans for their employment made the decision that was to bring the recruits both praise and obloquy by organising them into an anti-riot force that would trade blow for blow, and with interest!

As policemen the newcomers were novices but as shock troops they might well prove superb. And, should fears of the worst be realised and mob violence break out, 'shock troops' would be in very great demand.

O'Keeffe and his colleagues were told that the school was being split into two groups each about forty strong, slightly larger than an army platoon. They would be highly mobile and restricted to no particular district, and would be called on to 'break' disorder, wherever it appeared.

Such was the birth of what was to become famed in local lore as 'The Flying Column': condemned as 'Huns' by those at the receiving end of its fists, boots and staves, but lavishly praised by others as 'the Force that saved the City'.

At the time, however, the recruits were completely unaware that their new role was to achieve such historic significance. To O'Keeffe and his comrades it merely sounded exciting, and rather a lark as well . . .

If the strikers reported back for duty before eight o'clock they would be able to keep their jobs. As Salt started off on his travels he wished fervently that the authorities had thought fit to extend the deadline. But even had it been advanced to midnight there would scarcely have been the time to do what he wanted to do: namely, contact each striker individually and pass on the news of the limited 'amnesty' and the time of its expiry.

It was not that he had to go to the ends of the earth to find his colleagues. They all lived within a few streets of the station, and quite a few were next-door neighbours to each other. Trouble was, not all of them were at home, a fact that the Watch Committee seemed to have left out of its calculations.

One man was on the picket line, another in the boozer, a third was at a friend's house, discussing the situation, and others had left the city for the day, taking their families with them. Nor were the people he called on invariably appreciative of his efforts. Some indeed were positively hostile.

For Salt, acutely concerned by what he had heard regarding the apparent failure of the Strike and the need to get to the men to save their jobs, it was a frustrating experience to be rudely dismissed by one of them as a 'blackleg who has let his friends down'.

And in several cases his hearers just did not believe him when he said that the *Herald* had grossly distorted the picture of the response in other areas, particularly in its allegations of a mass walk-out in the 'Met'.

'It's a trick to get us back because they can't do without us and split the Union in two,' said a young PC. 'The bosses are trying to blind us with propaganda.'

But the unkindest and most hurtful cut of all was from a near-neighbour who just stared at him impassively, heard what he had to say and then, turning on his heel, still made no comment but slammed the door shut behind him.

Salt tried again, to be met this time by the man's wife. 'He's not talking to any of you traitors,' she said. 'He'll never speak to you again. He'd rather be fired than sell his mates like you've done.'

Before he could reply, the door had again slammed shut.

It almost made him feel ill, that brief, unpleasant incident, knowing as he did that the couple had three small kids to keep. Did they not realise the brave futility of their gesture he glumly wondered. Did they not know that the cause was already lost?

Through what remained of the sultry afternoon and early evening, Salt stubbornly continued in his task with varying fortune but considered at the end of it that it had been well worth while.

One woman had burst into tears of relief when he told her of the reprieve. Her husband, a PC of long service, had 'come out' only because he had thought that another man, his friend for years, had joined the strikers. Then, when he found this was not so, it had been too late to remedy the matter, or so he thought, and he had since been grimly trying to resign himself to the consequences. With kids to worry about, he had not found this easy, and the speed with which he had got back into uniform would have done credit to a quick change artist in the circus.

In another case the PC involved had acted in a temporary fit of pique and Salt for one could not blame him. The man's wife had been taken seriously ill and, after giving the children breakfast and getting them to school, he had reported for duty in such a rush that he had forgotten to button up his top tunic pocket. For this — at the start of the Strike! — he had received a long harangue on the need for discipline until, stung to the quick by his Sergeant's jeers at his 'slovenly socialist turnout' he had angrily decided that he might as well live up to the role and join the 'socialist' strikers. 'I've been calling myself every type of a fool since then,' he explained. He, too, got back to his post before the deadline.

By the time Salt had completed his mission, 51 strikers – one Sergeant and 50 Constables – had returned to duty. He would have liked the figure to have been a lot higher: and, given more time, it would have been. Yet 51 jobs saved were better than none, he consoled himself a little wearily. Union loyalties were fine but wives and children had to be fed. The butcher, baker, candlestick maker – these would not wait for ever. But if only they had given him more time.

And now there would be the other side of the job to think about, the task of restraining the violence that would come with the fall of night.

'Commencing about 3 o'clock yesterday afternoon, members of the City Police Force began to come out in large numbers . . . from this point until tea-time the men were coming out swiftly, though constables were on duty at all the chief traffic points in the City. In Bishopsgate over 100 men on shift came out during yesterday afternoon.'

Sir William Nott-Bower, Commissioner of the City of London Police Force, had been caught out almost as badly as Sir Edward Henry during the September Strike. Like Henry he had discounted the warning signals of unrest and, also like Henry, had been away on holiday when the trouble broke. But this time, profiting from experience, he knew practically every movement of his men, and the *Herald*'s picture of them responding in 'large numbers' to the Strike call had merely aroused in him a bloody-minded annoyance mixed with well-bred scorn.

Todate the City Police strikers numbered precisely fifty out of a total force of 2,000, a proportion of only two and a half per cent; and it looked like staying that way. Bar a few prominent diehards led by Zollner, there were no enthusiasts for martyrdom in a cause where the only major issue left outstanding, now that the pay and pensions terms had been announced, was whether the Union should be replaced by the Federation. The 'outside influences' that had tried to sway the force to militancy in NUPPO's favour, had already received their answer in the

Bishopsgate skirmish. So just what was the *Herald* up to?

In the circumstances, Sir William could be excused for thinking that the newspaper was letting the sentiments of its heart and mouth take precedence over the sanctity of facts, but imaginative licence in the Strike's reportage was by no means confined to Labour's only national daily. A Tory contemporary, only the day before, had wishfully put the Met strikers' strength at 'fewer than 100', even though Macready himself was reporting five times that figure, and anticipating there might be a few hundred more to come.

'A joke,' said the *Herald* primly of its rival's lapse, 'which blunter men would call a lie.'

Certainly the *Herald*, whatever its shortcomings in reporting the City scene, was to show itself to be well enough informed when, on Friday evening, it turned its attention to the situation in Liverpool and found that: 'The Liverpool police have responded in large numbers to the call of their union leaders, and it was reported yesterday afternoon that 700 out of a total of 2,000 had already come.'

John Ford, however, was not among them.

'Nobody will be doing that duty,' he had been told on Thursday night when looking up the traffic control arrangements for the Landing Stage.

At the time, as a novice to the scene, he had felt sufficiently curious to ask the reason why, but the cryptic answer – 'You'll learn time enough' – had left him as foxed as before. Only now, twenty-four hours later, had the meaning behind the words become abundantly plain.

His mentor of the night before was nowhere to be seen. Neither were the other regulars who had introduced him to the beat. Almost to a man they were 'out' in support of the Strike that everybody but he – and, judging by the Press, the city fathers too – had seen coming a mile away, and had made preparations for. Nobody was on duty on the Landing Stage. And neither was anyone on duty in the docks around it. The warehouses along the Mersey had been left unguarded.

For Ford the day had seen a series of surprises, the first arising when, on his way to Hatton Garden, he had been stopped by two men in plain clothes and ordered to go home. They said the police were on strike, and they were on picket duty. If he liked, he could join them: otherwise he must go home.

'But I know nothing about a Strike,' he had protested with sincerity. 'And I just can't knock off because you tell me to.'

'You'll go back home, and quick!' said one of them. 'There'll be almighty trouble if you don't.'

But instead, he had brushed them aside and pressed on for the Garden, surprised – though relievedly so – that they had not followed him, and evading only narrowly another group of pickets on the way.

The next turn-up for the book was when, as he entered the station, he found himself addressed by no less than a Chief Inspector.

'Had much bother in getting here?' the latter asked. 'Only a little, sir,' he answered modestly.

'Good lad. Good lad. Now tell me . . .' Then had followed such a series of questions about the state of the streets outside, that the raw recruit, though flattered by such an implied compliment to his powers of observation, found himself impertinently wondering: 'But why ask ME? Surely the powers-that-be aren't all that flaming ignorant?'

After this informal interrogation he was sent to the parade-room, and told to await further orders; but the wait proved a long one, and the orders were slow in coming. The afternoon dragged on in an atmosphere of unreality. The place somehow seemed untidy.

The usual parades had been set, and quite a number of the regulars turned up at the usual times. But although these were in uniform – whereas the men on Strike were obliged to wear civilians – it soon became obvious that their attendance was for their own convenience only. They were restless, uncertain and in search of news.

Instead of going to their posts, they let it be known that first they must go to Transport House, to receive instructions. Nobody tried to detain them. Very few of them came back.

But if these potential strikers found that accurate news of the Strike was scarce and hard to come by, the loyalists felt themselves to be almost completely in the dark. Just how was the situation developing outside the stout walls of the Garden? Was it really as menacing as the Mayor appeared to anticipate? There were times when it seemed to the keyed-up men as though their superiors had got together in a conspiracy of silence. In fact the true explanation of the continuing lack of news was almost unbelievably simple. No one could keep them posted because nobody really knew.

Apart from the crop of rumours, thick as the leaves of autumn and even richer in colour, inevitable in such an unprecedented situation, all that HQ had to work on were the apprehensions of worried civilians, each forecasting that the tragedy would be on his very own doorstep, and the reports from scattered members of the CID sent to potential trouble spots as soon as the Strike began.

A few isolated assaults, a build-up of tensions in the Great Homer Street area, crowds far larger than usual around the dockland pubs, a pitch and toss school unashamedly conducted within yards of a local 'nick' . . . here indeed were pointers of trouble to come, but as yet no-one could be sure of where or what would be the flashpoint.

Bitter respect for the rough justice handed out by the city police was still serving to hold the underworld in restraint. Its bully-boys were, so far, merely probing, feeling their way. Only when they had assured themselves that the Strike was really widespread, and the coppers not likely to return to the beat, would they dare to act. As yet they still could hardly believe their luck.

It was nearly eight o'clock before the first firm information came to hand that the lull was about to end. A crowd of out-of-works and shawlies had been gathering in the dockland estate for the past hour or so: now they were all on the move, towards the Sandon Dock.

Ford and ten other Constables were bundled into a patrol van and, with an Inspector in command, were sent to stop them.

They went in the back way, through the dock estate and left the van beneath the overhead railway. As they did so they heard for the first time the hullabaloo raised by the mob. Men, women and even some ragged children were laughing, jeering, yelling their heads off; a bank holiday crowd gone mad. And, mixed with their drunken uproar was a duller, more rhythmic sound. For a moment Ford could not quite place it, but then it came back to him: it was the thudding of axes on timber. They were trying to batter down the dock gate.

Unseen behind the tall walls that flanked it, the recruits lined up with staves in hand, while the Inspector, shouting through a gap in the planks, tried to make himself heard above the din; but nobody listened. His warnings of arrest sounded pretty thin to the rioters and served only to goad them on. The dock warehouses were bursting at the seams with everything they wanted, and only this one man, or so it seemed, stood in their way. A lifetime's loot could be theirs for the taking. He had better shut up.

'Bloody scuffer. Shut your gob!' The cry was taken up with embellishments, and became a chant. 'Shut your gob, or we'll shut it for you!'

Ford licked his lips, which had suddenly gone dry. There must be hundreds of the bastards; hundreds against eleven of them.

He caught a glimpse of an iron claw, groping through the aperture beneath the massive hinges, and heard the tortured sound of splintering wood.

'It's bloody crowbars now!' said the PC at his side.

Fresh splintering, followed by a roar of triumph as the gate began to give.

'I warn you!' yelled the Inspector, trying again, but his words were drowned by catcalls, and the gate suddenly burst open. There was the briefest of pauses and then the mob surged forward. The PCs emerged from concealment to meet them face to face.

So this was it! Ford felt his apprehension vanish, and fierce disgust and hatred take its place. Dock rats reeling like ships in a storm from the drunken spite within them, and brandishing a weaponry of axes, sticks, and crowbars ... a pack of wild women, hair streaming over shawled shoulders, ready to back them with their talons, grasping bricks and broken bottles ... rodents, bloody rodents every one of them, and the detachment's only hope was to move fast in putting them down!

For a tenth of a second Ford could sense – and savour – the crowd's shock at seeing the Inspector was not alone. Then came the order to charge, and everything else was forgotten.

It was no time for niceties. The odds against the police recruits were too great for them to follow a strict observance of the rules, and they did not even bother to try.

As they tore into the mob they laid about them in all directions, using their staves like flails to clear a way.

One man, attempting to stand his ground, went down like a pole-axed bull, blood spilling over his stubbled head and massive neck from a blow by one of Ford's companions, an ex-soldier completely unversed in more conventional police methods of restraint.

Another of the rioters hurled an axe at a charging PC with such force that, only narrowly missing its target, it lodged itself in the cement between the bricks of the dock wall. But then it was HIS turn to go under, and be encouraged to stay there by a regulation boot.

It was soon over. Sobered and appalled by the desperate wrath of the eleven, the rest of the crowd scattered, running back through the gateway and, as they did so, the police pursued them, still hitting out. Only after repeated blasts on his whistle, and a few angry words as well, was the Inspector able to recall them from the chase, and cool their fighting frenzy.

'Sore, sorry and surprised,' was the way that Ford was later to describe the state of the prisoners taken by the rush. They were still confused as to how their plans had come unstuck so quickly and it took time for them to realise that their opponents had been so few.

'We were told you bastards were out on strike,' said one man bitterly.

'You can always make a formal complaint about it,' the Inspector answered, deadpan.

The recruits came stumbling back and fell into rank. They were breathless, somewhat sheepish, yet proud of themselves notwithstanding. The first skirmish had been won. They had drawn – literally – first blood. It had not been a bad effort in the heat of a summer's evening – not for raw new boys, outnumbered thirty to one. 'But don't think you've got the night's work over with,' the Inspector warned them. 'There'll be a lot more of it to come.'

'There is going to be no nonsense about this. They have had their fair warning, and the men who come out must abide by the consequences.'

While the recruits from the Garden were having their moment of glory in the Liverpool docks, Shortt down in Whitehall was taking the opportunity of re-emphasising that this time there would be no repetition of the events of the year before. There would be no second thoughts on the part of the Government regarding its determination to destroy the Union, and no mercy would be offered to the strikers.

Up to the present, he revealed, only 854 men of the Metropolitan Police Force had failed to report for duty. All 854 had been dismissed, and an official notice to that effect would be published the following day. Not one of them, however great his merit in the past, would be reinstated.

This adamant refusal of the authorities to compromise on the dismissal issue had been demonstrated in an exchange in the Commons when Labour MP Frederick Roberts had tried to move an amendment to the Police Bill.

Roberts' purpose was to delete Clause 3 of the Bill whereby a police officer convicted and fined for causing 'disaffection' in the service, would also lose his pension rights and be barred from reinstatement. This, as he argued with some reason, had the effect of punishing a man twice over for the same offence.

Answering for the Government, Major Baird said that the offence 'was all the greater when committed by a policeman, who enjoys all the benefits of pension rights which are a reward for good service.' He had then gone on, amid protests, to describe the police strikers as 'mutineers'.

But Shortt, in reply to a similar attempted amendment by another Labour member, Tyson Wilson, went even further than Baird in the field of vituperation by claiming that any man convicted under the clause was a 'traitor'. There could be no question of such a man ever again being employed by the police, the Home Secretary insisted.

The amendment was withdrawn, and the Bill read a third time.

Macready, too, had stressed that there would be no dilution of the harsh medicine he had prescribed on 30 May for the Metropolitan force. Although it is probable that he regarded the dismissal issue not so much an instrument of punishment for those already 'out' as a weapon to deter others from following their example.

As he saw it the only thing that could spread the Strike, which he was otherwise convinced was doomed to failure, was the fear among the rank and file of Union 'reprisals', already threatened by Marston; and now by Hayes as well.

Even in the September Strike – 'popular' though it was – many a man had left the beat solely because of the threat that he would otherwise go down on the Union's records as a blackleg and be treated as such. This time such potential waverers must realise that whatever the Union might do to them, the authorities could go one better – or rather, worse – and would certainly do so. The best stiffener against fear was an even greater fear.

The Commissioner was equally calculating in his moves to scotch the Union's other ally – public panic at the consequences of a Strike. Assuming an air of complete indifference to the Strike organisers' shrill claims of success, he emphasised to the Press that the situation was under control, 'indeed very satisfactory'. The Strike had been very feeble, 'even more feeble than I had anticipated'. And finally, to make it clear that he really meant what he said, he boldly committed himself to a statement that he had no intention of suspending leave, or of calling upon the special constables to undertake the duty performed by the regular police. It would not be necessary.

In Liverpool they envied Macready his calm assurance, a quality they unfortunately could not share. For London the crisis appeared to be nearly over. In Liverpool it was only just beginning.

CHAPTER NINE

Battle Honours

'The Head Constable appeals to household and property owners to take steps individually for the safety of their property as he is not in a position to afford such protection as he would like . . .'

However slow he may have been in appreciating the steady build up of grievances among the men under his command, and the way in which those grievances would drive them to mass revolt, now that the revolt was in progress, Caldwell was quick enough to anticipate its effect on the city's peace.

He wanted to make sure that the public anticipated it too, though 'such protection as he would like' was a fairly mild substitute for what, measured against his resources, could have been rendered as 'hardly any protection at all'. He did not want a panic; merely that people should help themselves.

Caldwell had prepared his appeal while the strikers were holding a mass meeting in St George's Hall as a preliminary to a 'recruiting march' through the city centre.

Although this was solely for the purpose of inducing a change of heart among those still remaining loyal, he feared it was likely to have the undesired effect of impressing the city's undesirables with the size of the walk-out and the fragility of what remained of the forces of law and order. He decided to issue a strong call for 'public-minded citizens' to enrol as special constables.

Now, half-way through Friday night, he was only slightly cheered by the news of the mob's repulse at Sandon Dock and the fact that, bar a score or so of smashed windows and the looting of four shops, incidents had been comparatively light. By tomorrow the underworld would have got the full measure of the weakness of the police, and would act accordingly, the fickle populace of the slum lands rising with them.

Even should the specials, unacquainted with the brutal idiosyncrasies of the mob and completely untrained in police work, reach their target strength on time, it would be impossible for them to maintain the city's peace.

Aware of this, the Mayor had already taken the precaution of enlisting the support of the local garrison commander, but the force immediately available consisted of less than 700 men, drawn from variegated base units, and as inexperienced as the raw specials in the techniques of crowd control. The soldiers could easily be lost in the maze of side streets and alleys that made up the dock estates, and Liverpool 8 – a fortress city in itself – while there would also be the need to guard the hard cases in Walton Prison against possible rescue bids by their friends outside. Add to this the task of protecting other key points, docks, railway stations, power plant, post offices and the banks, and 700 soldiers would go nowhere.

'The Tommies haven't a hope,' said one of the Inspectors, a man with long experience of the violence of Liverpool's mobs and mobsters. 'Once the trouble starts, thousands will join in – just for the devil of it.'

Caldwell agreed. Should the army seek to protect every potential trouble spot, the troops would be thin on the ground, split up in small detachments, and highly vulnerable to an attack by the mob. If they did not use their weapons, they were likely to be overwhelmed. If they did use their weapons there would be a bloody massacre.

The thought was horrifying, and it was while Caldwell was considering its implications that the news came in from Great Homer Street, that was to be a foretaste of far worse to come.

'Don't think you've got the night's work over with,' the Inspector had said.

Ford and his fellow police recruits could not say that they had not been warned.

No sooner had they thought that they could relax after their Sandon victory than they were ordered into the van again and told of a new task. Trouble was expected in the adjacent Bramley Moore Dock, where ships were being loaded with food and other necessities from the USA for distribution in defeated Germany.

An informant had given the tip-off that certain well-known villains had got a crowd together to raid the place. Once again there had been an urgent SOS for the detachment to intervene.

But when they arrived at the Dock they had found it quieter than the grave. News of the sharp lesson that had been handed out to the mob at Sandon had been quick to circulate, and the appropriate moral drawn. The gang which had been preparing to lead and manipulate the crowd had decided it would be best to try its luck elsewhere.

'Think we'll have time for a break now, and a sup of tea and a sandwich?' enquired one of the more hopeful recruits as they drove back to HQ. The answer was a disappointment: a call to Sturla's, the big department store in Great Homer Street, dividing line in the old familiar battlefield between the Irish of the Orange and the Irish of the Green. Now, it would appear, this was Tom Tiddler's ground for the worst of both Irish factions.

This time, only six of the group were called for. Ford was among them but the man in charge was Inspector Paddy Marshall of D Division, a 'character' known locally and case-hardened to handling trouble. With this huge, bushy-whiskered personality to lead them they felt more than compensated for their lack of numbers. No matter how many villains might be waiting for them, it would be rough luck for any who got in Marshall's way.

Yet instead of the expected punch-up their mission ended on a note of anti-climax. When they reached the store it was to find that the mob had done all that it had set out to do and, laden with loot, had departed.

It was astonishing sight – what was left of this once prosperous department store. Ford would have thought it a traveller's tale, if he had not seen it himself.

Everything – but everything! – that was movable in the place had been removed, and an orgy of vandalism had destroyed everything that was not. Light fittings, show cases, and dummies

— all had been reduced to rubble, while even the window frames had vanished with the mob. They had stripped the store as clean as locusts loosed on a field of grain.

As the police recruits walked awed among the ruins, their heels dug into a sea of broken glass and their nostrils were filled with dust. They had anticipated that most of the stock would have been stolen, but for the mob to have removed the store's carpeting as well took them quite aback: for sheer fast-working efficiency Liverpool looters took quite a lot of beating.

Briefly Marshall surveyed the scene, pondered on a house-to-house check-up, and then gave up.

'Nobody will know a bloody thing,' he said, speaking his thoughts aloud. 'They never do. It's more than their lives are worth to be labelled as informers.'

Not a soul stirred in the street. Not a light was showing. The flats above the shops were in virtuous darkness. Great Homer Street stayed divorced from what had happened.

With nothing left for the squad to do except report on what they had found, Marshall decided to take them back to Hatton Garden. With two exceptions — Ford and one other. They were 'to keep an eye on things' — just what they could not imagine — and wait for the arrival of the manager, who should by now have been alerted. If they had any trouble with the locals — 'not that I think you will' — they were to stand no nonsense, but lash out with their batons. 'Show them who's boss' was the Inspector's parting injunction.

The vigil that followed his departure was a lonely one, and somewhat eerie too. A long wait enlivened only by the hope that some of the marauders might come back and try and mix it: but they did not. The street stayed deathly still. Occasionally a curtain stirred but that was all. They were being watched and knew it. But all was quiet.

It was not until 2 am that the manager arrived, with a police Sergeant as his escort. He was a bustling, rather self-important figure of a man, until he saw the wilderness that the mob had made of his empire and then to their consternation he broke down in tears.

133

Embarrassed, Ford looked away while the Sergeant tried to get him to pull himself together, but it just did not work. The man was in really deep distress and would not be comforted. Even when he was told there was nothing more they could do, he continued with his weeping.

He was still crying when they left.

Tears – tears by the bucketful were to be shed in Birkenhead before the week-end was out. Relieved by the announcement on Friday morning that the town's police force had rejected the strike call, though by a narrow margin, the *Post* had commented that, had this not been so, 'the community, indignant at the betrayal of its interest by the police, would undoubtedly have taken measures and very thorough measures to protect itself. More, the existing police force might have been superseded, and one in which the public could securely confide installed in its place.'

When darkness fell this prediction had a very hollow ring. The police had reversed their decision. The looters had come out in force. And the community's 'thorough measures' to protect itself proved, at that stage, non-existent.

The trouble had started earlier in the evening when 200 Liverpool strikers, joined by a host of supporters from the docks and transport unions, had marched to the unguarded pierhead and taken the Mersey ferry. Infuriated by the news that the Birkenhead men were not coming 'out' as expected, they were determined to make them change their minds, and when men of the night shift turned up for duty at Branden Street police station they found their way barred by a massive picket line, several hundreds strong.

Two of the women police were the first to be stopped. As they tried to force their way through the crowd they found themselves hemmed in by demonstrators from the Union seeking to convert them. After some mutual badinage, mostly good-natured, the girls were allowed to proceed. But others, their male colleagues, were less fortunate. There were scuffles here and there and an exchange of blows as they attempted to thrust through to the station. In the face of so much hostility some of the weaker-nerved

134

gave up and went home.

For those already mustered on the parade-ground the situation was confused, and the clash of loyalties strong. On the one hand, they were constitutionally correct in continuing with their duties, the vote in favour of a strike having failed to provide the two-thirds majority required by the Union's rule book. On the other, was the fact that the Union's leadership had called for strike action, and their colleagues in the Liverpool force were loudly accusing them of 'ratting'. They fidgeted uneasily, uncertain of themselves and of what they should do.

Then suddenly as if to bring matters to a head, several of the men who had voted for strike action during the morning's meeting, but had agreed to abide by the decision of the ballot, broke rank and, calling on the rest to follow, dashed across to join the picket line. From the crowd, swollen by locals anxious to see the fun and play the 'scuffers' off against each other, came a roar of applause.

For a few moments longer the loyalists continued to endure their state of indecision, until an Inspector arrived, and attempted to end it. Worried by the unsettling effect of the delay he formed the men up in twos and placing himself at their head, marched them out of the gate, and straight towards the crowd.

It was a bold move and one that could have led to a head-on clash. But the strikers themselves fell back, and the 'outside elements' that would have welcomed a confrontation had to fall back, too, restrained by their allies.

But it was also a move that was to have an unexpected side effect. Once marched to their posts, the men were isolated and thus more open than ever to 'persuasion'. Within the next hour or so, sixty Birkenhead men – a quarter of the total force – had joined the Liverpool strikers, while others were besieged in the station or their homes.

Late though this development was, the locals were quick to snatch their opportunity. Born in poverty, constantly in debt, their first thought, appropriately, was to pay a visit to the pawnshop – which they stripped of its contents while calling hospitably to passers-by to join in and share their good fortune. There was plenty for everyone, they said, and the police were all on strike; an exaggeration that was to mean two months' hard labour for two of the many taking advantage of the offer. Loyal constables caught them dallying on the site after the rest of the crowd had vanished.

However, for the remainder involved in the pawnshop raid it had been a vastly successful venture, inspiring them to loot three more shops before the night was out, and it was expected that once the news got around more Birkenhead citizens would follow their example during the night to come. Saturday night was going to be something special, it was said. A chance of settling old scores, redeeming pledges and making a handsome profit in the process.

For most Londoners the morning of Saturday, 2 August was something special, the start of the first peacetime bank holiday for five years, and the Police Strike made little impact on the crowds thronging Waterloo and Victoria railway terminals, determined to enjoy themselves. Most of the national dailies were celebrating the failure of the strike in the capital, with only the *Herald* striking a discordant note and expressing its fear that the Police Bill's provisions against 'disaffection' could also mean the muzzling of the Press.

'Under the Bill,' said its leader writer, 'not only will such a strike as the present police strike be illegal, an article such as this will be illegal. It will be illegal for anyone to express sympathy with any grievance of the police.'

In Liverpool, however, the local newspapers were more concerned with the action that was currently taking place before their eyes, than the implications of the Government's legislation on the future of Press freedom.

The morning's *Liverpool Daily Post* featured prominently Caldwell's call for volunteers for the specials to enrol before 6 pm, and there was also news of an appeal for extra troops, some of whom were expected to arrive that afternoon. To most of its readers the *Post's* revelations came as a big surprise, conjuring up as they did the control of local streets by men in steel helmets with bayonets fixed. Was the situation really so serious as to require such intervention? Typically English in their approach to anything outside the usual norm, many doubted it.

In the Bridewell at Rose Hill, however, the scene was sufficiently abnormal to have convinced even the greatest sceptic that the city was going through dangerous times. The corridors and parade-room were littered with clothes, mattresses, chairs, bedsteads and bedclothes – loot of all kinds reclaimed in clashes with pillagers during the night. So many arrests had been made that the cells were unable to contain the prisoners. Men and women were being booked all the time. Considering its skeleton strength, the city police force was doing remarkably well on the detection side of its brief; in prevention, however, it had been decidedly weak. The manager of Sturla's was not the only one to mourn the ruin of his livelihood by the mob.

For Ritchie the position was particularly worrying. He had been delighted by the response to his emotional appeal to the police recruits in Hatton Garden. Predictably, they had been unable to protect anything but a relatively small proportion of shops and businesses in the danger areas, but their keenness and toughness in action had held the mob back from even worse outrages and had deterred others from joining in. All the same, the recruits' preliminary successes had been achieved against crowds largely disorganised, and probably only a fraction of those who would shortly go on the rampage, and the damage already inflicted on the property owners of Liverpool 8 boded ill for the bill that the week-end would bring.

And now, to add to Liverpool's problems, had come the alarming news from Birkenhead and Bootle: neighbours who had caught the city's infection and caught it badly. Only yesterday Ritchie had praised the former's police force for its 'sense of responsibility' in deciding not to strike, yet now nearly half of that force had joined the strikers, the looting had begun, and there was fear of major rioting after nightfall.

Much though the situation in Birkenhead had soured, however, the position of the Bootle force was even worse. Of a total strength of 110 officers and men, only 16 remained at their posts and – whereas the Mersey separated the city from Birkenhead – Bootle projected into Liverpool's groin. The ill-disposed could be expected to make the most of this geographical opportunity.

As the Mayor saw it, and Caldwell concurred with his view, the Birkenhead and Bootle defections could have a serious effect on the city itself. What military resources would normally have been made available to it would now have to be spread through the neighbouring towns as well, while the law-breakers would have doubled their support. And should disaffection take hold of other provincial forces, and the soldiers be stretched even thinner on the ground, the possibilities of a shooting incident would be high indeed. The prospect was indeed a frightening one.

For the police strike and its possible consequences to Liverpool could not be considered in isolation from the scenario of conflict that, although its gravest overtones were registered in the industrial north-west, was currently agitating the country as a whole.

There was a crisis in the mines and a crisis on the railways. There was a bakers' strike in progress, and a strike threatened on the city's tramways. Unemployment was rife and promised to get even worse. The Discharged Soldiers and Sailors Federation was just one of several extremist groups currently whipping up the demobbed masses, bitterly disillusioned by their reception in 'the land fit for heroes to live in'.

Nor was the prevailing discord in what had been a united nation confined to domestic issues; it embraced foreign affairs as well. Increasingly, trade union leaders were expressing, in the names of their members, discontent over what they called the 'suppression' in Ireland and India and, with particular vehemence, the allied intervention in Russia. There were calls for 'direct action' in the form of demonstrations and strikes, for political rather than industrial reasons and, in counterpoint, demands for a strong reaction that rivalled those in Italy made by an up-and-coming Mussolini.

Lloyd George is said to have claimed that Britain had never been nearer bolshevism than it was at the time of the 1918 Police Strike. In Liverpool, almost a year later, they felt the threat was even nearer. A single shot by a nervous or angry young soldier might well be followed by a fusillade, rousing echoes that would reverberate through every home in the country.

To prevent such a tragedy it was essential to keep the city's trouble localised by deploying against each incident as it arose, troops, specials, and non-striking police regulars in such numerical strength that firearms would not be necessary. Of course, this was easier said than done.

With his own military background to guide him, Ritchie could see all too clearly the problems involved in a commander having to switch his scanty forces rapidly from one threatened trouble spot to another when their route lay along narrow streets flanked by the yards and alleys of a community that was traditionally hostile to both the army and the law. The young soldiers would have to proceed on foot, subject to insult and attack and a multitude of delays, exhausting not only of time but of nerves and tempers too. In such circumstances lay the seed for trigger-happiness.

But while the Watch Committee were at one in agreeing that to avoid a take-over of the city by the mob or a massacre of the mob by the army it was essential that replacements for the police should be strong and prompt in arriving, the question requiring an answer was – where were they to come from?

When large-scale confrontations had arisen in the past the city fathers had been able to make their plans in the secure knowledge that their police could be augmented by strong contingents from the police forces of other areas, however far removed: Birmingham police, for example, had played an important if controversial role during the riots of Bloody Sunday. For obvious reasons there could be no such reinforcement now.

Nor could the War Office, its regular manpower strained by the Irish commitment and a residue of wartime conscripts increasingly clamorous for demob, do very much more than it was doing at the moment. More cities than Liverpool might yet require its help.

It was at that moment, however, while they were desperately seeking, and not finding, additional resources, that Ritchie came up with a suggestion that, for simplicity and novelty, captured the imagination of them all, including Maxwell: the navy. Why did they not call in the navy?

The Senior Service, the Mayor pointed out, was known to provide technical teams for use against situations threatening to life or property. Men had been sent to man the pumps and keep the pits from flooding – during the recent pit strike, for example. But he had something in mind that was rather more ambitious. Shore-based sailors from the depots, or even one of the smaller units of the fleet would only be of limited use in the crisis faced by the city. So why not ask for the largest, most impressive item in the navy's armoury? Why not ask for a battleship?

A battleship; Ritchie, having made up his mind on the need for naval assistance, had certainly decided to do it in style.

But a battleship on the Mersey, he reasoned, could well change the whole pattern of events within the city. Not only was there an excellent chance that its show of force might serve to overawe the malcontents and enforce the *Pax Britannica* by implication rather than by violent action: it could also provide a handy base for action should its deterrent factor fail. The army would be confined in its activities by the intricate geography of the streets, but the navy would have the broad river as its highway.

Moored off the Pierhead, the ship would be placed to send, at minutes' notice, landing parties of blue-jackets and marines to operate on either bank while her boats, patrolling the river, could isolate the city's rioters from those of Birkenhead. And last, but by no means the least important of the considerations that had guided him in his choice, there was the question of what, today, would be known as public relations. The navy, with its image of Jolly Jack, was dear to many hearts, whereas the army was not. So a battleship it must be.

Amid some excitement it was agreed that the Mayor should contact the Home Office and ask for official backing for Liverpool's request. Top Admiralty clearance would be necessary for any switch in the navy's resources. Battleships, like money, did not grow on trees.

No record exists of the feelings with which the civil servants in Whitehall initially received the Mayor's unexpected request, made over the telephone on that working Bank Holiday Saturday. Their reactions can only be surmised; the situation was quite unorthodox.

But the vision projected by Ritchie of the benefits arising from a naval intervention was evidently sufficiently convincing to make a big impression on Shortt. He promptly promised his assistance in the task of turning it into a reality, and ordered his office to make an immediate approach to the Admiralty.

There, however, the project not only ran into heavy weather, but briefly appeared endangered by torpedo action too.

'Are you certain that all this is really necessary?' The Home Office civil servant found the Duty Commander at the Admiralty unenthusiastic to the extent of being positively unhelpful.

Traditionally, the navy had always been reluctant to become involved in civil controversy. Currently it had serious problems of its own. Demobilisation was not proceeding fast enough to please the fleet's massive intake of wartime entrants, and there was grave discontent on the lower deck over the pay issue as well.

But probably helping to stiffen the Duty Commander's reluctance was the fact that, unbeknown to the Home Office and beleagured Liverpool, the Admiralty lines were still buzzing with the repercussions of an eager officer's compliance with a far more modest request for aid. One that had come from Southampton only the week before.

Faced with a strike by corporation employees, and fearing the prospect of a breakdown in the local sewage system, the city's mayor had appealed to the local RN depot for a detachment to help keep the pumps working. Unfortunately, however, neither His Worship nor the officer temporarily in charge of the depot, Lieutenant Commander Sir George Johnstone Bart, RNVR, realised that, in the quick agreement that followed, they had committed what amounted to a cardinal sin. They had by-passed 'the normal channels'. They had not consulted Whitehall.

Thus while the arrival of the ratings at the pumps was welcome news to the population of the city at large, its Nelsonian preference for action over precedent evoked no joy in the corridors of the Admiralty. Instead the reaction there had been one of near-incredulity and dismay. Could it be that Sir George, without so much as a by your leave, had committed the navy to intervene in an industrial dispute? If so, his conduct would have dangerous political implications. Say that his blue-jackets should be dubbed as blacklegs and strike-breakers?

'Is it a fact that naval ratings have been employed since last Saturday in connection with a local dispute between the Corporation and its employees? If so, report full details.'

Returning from leave, the Senior Naval Officer, Southampton, was greeted by a terse signal marked 'Urgent', and signed by no less an authority than the First Sea Lord. Rallying to his subordinate's aid, the SNO explained that the mayor had feared that a large, low-lying area of the town might be flooded with sewage if the pumps remained unmanned, and a severe epidemic could well have followed. But this was not good enough for the Admiralty, which still refused to be placated. More information was demanded about 'the effects of this officer's unauthorised action'.

'I have pointed out to Lieutenant-Commander Johnstone the possible serious consequences which may accrue from the intervention in local labour troubles of naval ratings without the proper authority,' the SNO signalled back, but more than this guardedly-phrased admission of rebuke was needed to assuage the First Sea Lord's righteous anger.

He had sent his Chief of Staff to visit the scene in person, and it was only when the latter had reported back that, far from there being hostility between the seamen and the strikers they were on very good terms with each other and had reached a compromise on their respective activities, did authority relent. It had then been agreed that no further disciplinary action be taken against the luckless Johnstone. His 'narrow squeak' was an awful warning of the perils inherent in meeting the most innocuous of appeals, and it was indeed small wonder that the Duty

Commander's reaction to Liverpool's call on the navy should have been so cool.

If the dispatch of 47 ratings to work a few sewage pumps for a city menaced by plague had caused such a furore among the Admiralty's top brass, just how unwelcoming would their reaction be to this new appeal?

The navy was being asked to send a battleship to what was currently the UK's most explosive trouble-spot. Worse, by being asked specifically to put on a show of force it would, in effect, be committing its ratings to take the place of the police strikers, backed by some of the most eloquent and most militant radicals in both Parliament and the TUC. Grimly the Duty Commander forecast squalls ahead.

Nor were the objectors to the move, once news of it got around, composed solely of those apprehensive of its political implications. The Fleet was not accustomed to having its components whistled up at will by panicking civic authorities, and battleships were costly things to move. The navy was currently in the grip of an economy campaign as regards its oil and coal. There was also the question, put purely in passing, as to who would foot the bill.

However, by then Shortt had won his battle, although – reportedly – it had come as a big surprise to him that he had been obliged to fight it. He had come up against a stubbornness almost equal to his own and, even though unaccustomed to opposition and impatient of criticism, had had to invoke the weight of the Cabinet and the Deputy Prime Minister to overcome the Admiralty's objections. But overcome them he had, and the navy, too magnanimous to bear grudges, had not only provided him with a battleship, but a battleship that was one of the most recent and most powerful in the Fleet. HMS *Valiant*.

Belleisle, Havana, the two Ushants and the Saintes, the Glorious First of June, and Groix, 1795 . . . the battle honours associated with the *Valiant*, aptly named, dated from the era of the 'wooden walls' to the steel-turreted guns of Jutland, in a catalogue of action from the Spanish Main to the bleak North Sea.

Following such a roll of glory, 'Pierhead, Merseyside' may have appeared to those aboard the ship to be more than a little mundane. Yet there, as elsewhere, the *Valiant* was to deserve well of her country.

Whatever the initial dissatisfaction that had greeted her current employment, the ship's company had determined to make the best of things. Shortt, now that the die had been cast, would be given no cause to gripe.

And on the shore, meanwhile, O'Keeffe and his fellow recruits of the Flying Column were earning 'battle honours' too. The Scotland Road, the London Road, Great Homer Street; though their setting was unromantic the honours were arduously won.

By the time that Shortt was able to assure Ritchie that fresh army reinforcements were on the way, and that his longed-for battleship was steaming south from Scapa, 'The Men who Saved the City' were already engaged in close combat against those disturbing the city's peace. There were quite a lot who fitted into this latter category, though only a few hundreds could be fitted into the local jails.

CHAPTER TEN

Of Mourning and Mayhem

Increasingly bored with their austere surroundings and impatient for more active and belligerent a role, the recruits who had been mustered in Hatton Garden had to wait for their first chance of real action until early on Saturday night, when one of the two squads into which they had been divided was alerted to squash a riot, raging in London Road.

O'Keeffe was one of those involved in this confused and bloody affair though, as he was habitually to stress, 'in a purely unofficial capacity'.

The theory behind the organisation of the Column was that while one squad would be on call, to go wherever needed, the other would rest in reserve, being put on readiness only on the other's return. But the chance to try their hand at mixing it with the mob proved irresistible to O'Keeffe and several others with him in the 'resting' squad, so they tagged on to the departing duty men, adding a third to their strength.

However, the bosses indulgently turned blind eyes to this blatant disregard for police orders, and both O'Keeffe and his friend, John Harrison were subsequently to find themselves in the forefront of the battle.

The first blow of the many that were to give the Scotland Road a national notoriety was struck in the early evening when the windows of Latarche, family jewellers, were stove in by a pack of youngsters and, as if at a pre-arranged signal, the mob abandoned its attitude of watchful waiting, threw off its leash, and came snarling on to the streets.

At the sound of the shattering of the glass the road seemed to fill with people, running out of pubs, homes, and side alleys, to join in competing for the loot. Soon the shop was surrounded by a crowd that was ten yards deep. From it came not a single word of protest.

Silverware, watches and rings were grabbed by the gang who had staged the initial break-in: the others, who had followed them, cleared the place in minutes of the rest of its contents. Next, neighbouring shops of humbler style became the targets of the mob. Tobacconists, a tailor's, a furniture store, were smashed into, and looted.

To one terrified witness of the affair, 'it was as if the sea had overwhelmed us. The women went for the clothes shops, the men for the pubs and whisky stores. The children went for the sweet-shops. And that was only the start of the district's troubles . . .'

By the time the reinforcements from the Garden reached the scene the rioting had reached a particularly savage stage. A distillery had been broken into and drunken revellers were attempting to start a bonfire. Looters, though already surrounded by small mountains of their swag, were looking for still more. And some men with iron bars were smashing shop windows and doors without even bothering to enter the premises, content to wage destruction for destruction's sake. Like Ford and the detachment at Sandon Dock the night before, O'Keeffe and his colleagues set to work with an angry will.

It was a good night for the baton, used quite ruthlessly. The men had been told that, should the riot spread, the whole city could erupt, and they needed no prompting as to what was best to do. Their objective was not so much to take prisoners as to dole out punishment – break the mob up.

But although, at first, they seemed to be succeeding admirably in their task, with the crowd scattering in fright before each charge, and dropping much of its plunder in the process, a flaw soon appeared in the pattern of their success. No sooner had they cleared a space in one section of the street, than the crowds would re-form again, to attack and plunder another. Fit though he was, O'Keeffe was soon quite breathless with it all.

It was now becoming clear that the numbers against which the column was pitting its strength were not lessening, but increasing. For every rioter who, impressed by the baton charges, had decided to go home, there were one or more replacements, mostly coming from the pubs, and these men were a lot bolder than their predecessors. Hooligans who were looking for a fight rather than mere looters, they ripped cobblestones from the alleys to bombard the police as they re-formed. On three occasions O'Keeffe's helmet was knocked off, such was the force behind this hail of missiles – and each time he manoeuvred dazedly through the crush to pick it up again. He felt unprotected, almost naked, without his headgear: besides, he did not want the enemy to sport it as a trophy.

By midnight the London Road, despite the recruits' best efforts, was still a seething mass of rampaging humanity, adding with each surge towards the shops, a further contribution to the district's ruin. The Squad just was not big enough to tackle more than a part of it at once. Trouble, doused in one area, flared up minutes later in another.

At the end of a particularly heavy charge, with fists and batons raining blows in all directions as the squad came under a barrage of bottles, O'Keeffe was astonished to observe, before the next dash forward, a little group of men whom the night's looting, riots, and battle appeared to have completely passed by. While police and rioters clashed around them, these were squatting on the pavement and quietly minding their own business: indulging in the illegal game of pitch and toss.

He did not pinch them. He had not the time to pinch them. Nor, come to think of it, did he have the heart to do so. There were worse elements than gambling schools among the masses that filled the London Road that night. Yelling the only thing they knew, the war cries of the trenches, the squad once again returned to the attack.

Four of them, blowing off fumes and steam, they rumbled noisily and majestically over the tramtracks that led to the city centre, ground laboriously up the steep slope before St George's Hall and then, to the admiration and astonishment of the crowds outside Lime Street Station, settled down on their haunches, to dominate the plateau.

The navy had released a precious battleship for the city. The army, not to be outdone in generosity, had sent tanks, though few law-abiding Liverpudlians rapturously welcoming the arrival of these armoured reinforcements for the city's peace, appreciated the limited scope for their employment.

They were impressive brutes, with huge appetites: each of them swallowed a gallon of fuel per mile. They were hot-blooded brutes, with temperatures of 100 degrees, torturing the men in their bellies. But they were also, said a tank driver to a bystander, 'completely bloody useless for the job in hand'. The army, he added, wiping away the sweat, had sent a bloody sledge-hammer to crack a bleeding nut.

However, despite such reservations by the military, the Mayor and Corporation were happy enough to see these 'landships' – as someone had once described them – firmly anchored in the city's heart. Though destined, for the most obvious of reasons, never to move an inch against the rioters, the tanks fulfilled a vital role in publicising – and much exaggerating – the extent of the army's presence and commitment.

Restive businessmen, it was hoped, would gain reassurance from the sight of their massive hulls and bristling hardware. Villains would be appropriately subdued by this hint of the odds that, apparently, were being deployed against them. In short, the tanks would be of good propaganda value; and this at a time when the facts were dismally discouraging to 'authority'.

Among army reinforcements which had entered, or were due to enter the city over the week-end, the names of several famous infantry regiments featured prominently. The Sherwood Foresters, the Notts and Derby Regiment, the Leicesters and the Royal Welch Fusiliers . . . the tally of titles looked impressive in the extreme, but concealed very grave deficiencies. With the exception of the Fusiliers, none of the units concerned was at anything like battalion strength. They were, in fact, contingents drawn from their parent units and probably – though no figure was ever to be officially announced – the total strength of the troops involved never exceeded 2,500, many of whom were needed to protect the docks and civic buildings.

There was also a force of Hussars, dispatched from York, but the cavalry horses were unused to the stone setts of the Liverpool streets, and the troopers had to be lent the steeds that once had carried the city's mounted police.

It had always been accepted that the soldiers, hurriedly assembled as they were, would need time to re-group and be briefed before being committed to the work of riot-control, a field in which they were totally inexperienced. Their officers needed to concert plans with the police and civil authorities, and also to accustom themselves to the city's complicated geography.

But by late Saturday night, with the London Road – Scotland Road cauldron continuing to boil, it was decided that the hard-pressed police – regulars, recruits and specials – had taken about all that they could take from the mob.

So far, although so hopelessly out-numbered, they had managed to hold the pot from spilling its contents into the streets outside their thin protective cordon: but that cordon was beginning to bend; given the current pressure it could not be very long before it cracked and broke completely.

Reluctantly, and acutely aware of the nightmare risks involved in committing soldiers, trained to kill in battle, to the task of restoring civil peace, the authorities now decided they had no recourse but to bring forward the timing of their original plans, and send in the troops right away.

Farce and drama, good nature and brutality, both went hand in hand in the London Road as the rioting increased, embracing not only the small-time villains but all sorts of unlikely converts to their cause from the 'respectable' and well-breeched.

At one point the rioters had grown so bold that they switched on the electric lights of the shops they pillaged, while a group who had broken into one of the district's departmental stores started generously distributing the loot.

Ladies' mantles, blouses, stockings, dresses of all sorts were passed through the shattered glass of the window to a crowd of women 'shoppers', cheering as each 'gift' arrived and blowing kisses.

It was an almost festive occasion, but its brightness was quickly marred.

'For pity's sake stop this nonsense.' The speaker was an Australian soldier, just finishing his leave. Stepping in front of the happy crowd he pleaded with them to leave the place alone, adding with a courage far exceeding his discretion: 'There's some of you here who ought to know better. What would your husbands say?' There was an astonished pause in the excited chatter, and he was promptly hit on the head from behind with a slab of window sash and knocked unconscious.

Luckily for the Australian, he was known in the district and word of his plight reached the squad, at that time only a hundred yards away in neighbouring William Brown Street.

For O'Keeffe the occasion was memorable for its peculiarly eerie sequel. As he tried to close with one of the leaders of the looters, his boot hit an obstacle on the ground, and he stumbled and fell, to find himself embracing a naked woman! A naked woman moreover who was motionless and chill.

'It's a corpse,' he thought, terrified. 'They must have murdered her. I've collided with a corpse.' And then, still face to face with his frightening find, he took a second look, to realise with relief that the lady was a fake. 'She' was a female dress dummy, stripped of fol-de-rols and pitched into the street from an adjoining costumier's.

But then came the problem of getting to his feet. He seemed entangled with the wretched dummy, and his comrades were far too busy to offer him any help. Each time he tried to rise he was swiftly floored as the tide of battle ebbed and flowed above him. When he eventually succeeded in freeing himself he had the first good laugh of the night.

The rescue of the Australian had in fact made them all feel better. Their quick reaction had taken the looters by surprise, and the latters' casualties had been heavy in the fight that followed. While the recruits had sustained only cuts and bruises as a result of their attack, the enemy's wounds included cracked heads and fractured limbs.

However, those who dared think that they might have won a temporary breathing space were soon shown to be mistaken. There was still no let-up for the squad, merely a switch of incidents.

Even while they were rounding up the injured prisoners of their victory, preparatory to bundling them into a police tender, there came an SOS from another quarter, and then from another at the opposite end of the road. By the time that the soldiers arrived they scarcely had sufficient breath to raise a welcoming cheer.

The army had moved into the London Road with considerable style, throwing a cordon of steel-helmeted troops in battle order to the north and south of the riot area and marching them, line abreast, towards the centre. The police, exhausted, looked on with critical admiration.

They certainly looked business-like enough, these tidy men in khaki. With rifles at the port, bayonets fixed, they also had the advantage of looking extraordinarily lethal, an aspect that the mob was quick to appreciate.

Accompanying the troops was an armoured car but as the vehicle came to a halt it became clear that the machine gun projecting menacingly from its turret was to serve, on this occasion, a purely ornamental purpose. For suddenly the turret lid swung open and out climbed the well-known figure of a certain city magistrate notoriously unloved.

For a moment the crowd, curious as to the reason for this most unexpected visitation, paused in its clamour to let the man speak. But no sooner had he begun to read from the scroll he unfolded before him than their temper changed to fury. He was reading the Riot Act.

Nervously the magistrate rushed through his lines and then, with a volley of bricks and stones around his ears, he jumped gratefully back into his armoured refuge.

The battle was nearly over. As the troops moved slowly forward the crowds began to fall back, or else disappear into the numerous side streets that lay to the right and left of the line of advance. And, as they did so, the toll of the night's disorders, no longer part concealed by the milling crowds, was revealed in all its magnitude, a spectacle sufficient even to move the police to wonder.

Until now they had had no time in which to tot up the tally of destruction. Their impressions had been kaleidoscopic, one scene dissolving into another at every movement of the mob. The looted jewellers . . . the dummy 'corpses' . . . looters spilling their spoils as the police attacked . . . such encounters as these had been fragmentary, each fragment part of the pattern of the whole but, absorbed in the confusion of half a dozen bloody clashes, they had not even tried to put the pieces together. Not until now.

The entire length of the London Road was fringed with shattered glass, much of it turned into a glittering frost beneath the street lamps by the boots of police and rioters, pounding it into powder. Doors littered the paving stones, or else hung from torn hinges between gaping holes that once were windows, stripped of blinds and shutters by the cupidity of the crowd. The whisky distillery had been gutted, even its 'empties' having been used as amunition against the police. The nearby chewing gum factory had been stripped completely bare by a crowd that, so rumour went, had consisted largely of children. Even a tiny lock-up greengrocer's, empty of fruit though it was at the time of the attack, had not been spared . . . the three planks which constituted its counter had been smashed to pieces by the mob.

Yet, curiously, the aspects of this forbidding scene that were to live the longest in the memories of the recruits were trivial, almost casual in their nature; by-products of the destruction rather than the destruction itself.

The man on crutches whom they saw hobbling down the London Road, with a pair of boots in each hand and several more suspended from his neck . . .

The old lady who, appearing to be inordinately fat, was found to be wearing eight corsets over her dress, concealing them beneath her shawl . . .

And then there was the 'generous' looter who, having swag to spare, had kindly offered some of it to a needy-looking character – a CID man, who had booked him on the spot!

But while the antics of such characters were to be remembered by the Squad in many a reunion during the years to come, other far grimmer aspects of the crisis would be gratefully forgotten.

All the same, as the lull descended on the London Road that Saturday night, the memory of the violence of the mob was too recent to be so philosophically dismissed, and they prepared for fresh, perhaps greater aggravation on the morrow. Relieved at last, and returning to the station, they knew in their aching bones that this respite was only temporary, and could not possibly last. This was an armistice. It was not peace.

While O'Keeffe had started his eventful Saturday stint in the parade-room at Hatton Garden, Ford, after leaving the manager of Sturla's to his misery, had expected to rejoin the rest of the Squad and – happy thought – get some sleep.

Instead, the Sergeant had told him they were reporting to Rose Hill, where the Devil had more work for tired hands to do.

The majority of the prisoners taken during the night had been sent there. So had most of the pillaged property found abandoned on the streets. For its infinite variety this would have put Petticoat Lane to shame, but Ford had no chance to contemplate it at leisure; being sent out with detectives hopefully to find some more.

Their task involved searching a number of suspect homes and, by the time they had completed it, he was full of admiration for the unloved CID. For knowledge of their parish those tough characters were second to none.

Ignoring the injured protests of the locals, many of whom they addressed by their christian names, they had gone straight for the hiding holes that stored the plunder as if guided there by magnets. By the end of the search so much loot had been recovered that the recruits who wrapped it in sheets and tablecloths for transit to the Bridewell on their shoulders, looked more like glorified rag-gatherers than up-and-coming smart young policemen.

It was after 6 am when they got back to Rose Hill and received their first refreshment: a mug of coffee and a water biscuit, a somewhat stingy ration so they thought. But, although given so little sustenance for their bellies, at least they received a substantial pat on the back. This came from the formidable Superintendent Foulkes who, with rare amiability, went so far as to congratulate them on their labours and tell them that they were free to return to the Garden at last.

Moving in pairs, and at two minutes intervals – a device designed to help them outwit the Union pickets – they were back in the parade-room by 7.30: 'looking very unkempt, and as if we'd spent a month on the tiles.'

Compared with such a chronicle of activity the rest of the daylight hours had been relatively uneventful, and Ford had been able to get some rest by sleeping rough in the parade-room. Come dark, however, he had found himself involved in the closing stages of the London Road affair and it was nearly dawn before he had been able to close his eyes again. By then his tiredness had vanished and his brain was disgustingly lively, but he fought back all its temptations to linger on what he had seen and done and literally willed himself to go to sleep.

The mob would come back for more – he was absolutely sure of it – and it might be a long, long while before he got a spot of shut-eye again. So best make the most of it.

'The city is in a state of anarchy.' The phrase was strong, but John Corkhill, secretary to the Lord Mayor, felt as he penned it that it was an understatement.

When magistrates were obliged to read the Riot Act only to be answered by a shower of bricks and bottles, and were forced to take refuge in an armoured car . . . when criminals, thousands strong, rampaged through one of the city's major thoroughfares and held it for four hours of bitter fighting . . . when transport workers, dock workers, railway workers, and other unionist radicals were threatening to down tools in support of the Police Strike . . . then it seemed to the city fathers that their world had turned upside down.

Of Mourning and Mayhem

The success of the police recruits defending the docks on Friday night had been followed by a serious set-back on the Saturday. With almost every available policeman committed to the defence of the approaches to the city's heart, it had been dockland's turn to suffer from the exactions of mob rule; vast quantities of supplies newly landed from America were looted from the sheds of the Wellington Dock, and wholesale pillaging broke out in the others.

Nor was the prospect any brighter across the water in Birkenhead, where the police strikers now numbered 106, or over 70 per cent of the force's total strength. The horrors that had brought ruin to Liverpool 3 had been duplicated on the streets and waterfront of the town, requiring the intervention of troops originally assigned to the city itself.

But Corkhill's worries were not confined to the ravages, and potential ravages, of the mob alone. The Mayor's fear that other elements, motivated by revolution, might seek to profit from the crisis, had grown stronger as a result of the events of the night.

The victory of the forces of law and order, loudly acclaimed and welcome though it was, had been achieved with difficulty, and was certainly not decisive. Say, for instance, that the Irish republicans should decide to intervene and tilt the balance, turning the current situation into something immeasurably worse?

Far-fetched though the idea might have seemed in happier days, by the context of its time it had a powerful logic. Having succeeded in plunging Ireland into war, leading rebels were known to be eager to stage a big diversion in Britain itself. All they had lacked – so far – was the opportunity. Maybe they would consider they had that opportunity now. For what better choice of venue for these men than the policeless and strike-ridden city, housing in its sprawling working-class quarters so much ready-made support for the apostles of the republic by their fellow nationals of the 'Green'.

And lastly, to plague the authorities still further with the consequences that could follow a renewal of the violence, were the problems posed by the growing racial tension in the city. Liverpool's black minority was no recent phenomenen, but long-established. Preceding the invasion of the Irish, it dated back to Merseyside's eminence in the slave trade. But latterly, after decades of grudging but mainly peaceful co-existence, the relationships between the two communities had taken a sharp turn for the worse, culminating in a riot in which fugitive blacks, chased from their homes, had been rescued only by strong police intervention. What chance such intervention in the circumstances of today?

There was a definite feeling in the council on Sunday morning that Whitehall – despite its protestations of 'full support' – had very little conception of the magnitude of the special problems bedevilling the administration of an area so divided by religious, racial, and industrial disputes, and so extreme in its contrasts of vast wealth and grinding poverty.

'The City is in a state of anarchy,' Corkhill used the words advisedly. Maybe they would help spur London to action.

By the vast majority of the Liverpool community, trying to recover from the events of the night before, the police recruits of the Flying Column might well be regarded in the light of heroes, but to Jim Marston, grappling with the need to keep NUPPO alive, they were just like all other loyalists in the service: 'Caterpillars who haven't the nerve to come out on strike!'

The Union's President used the phrase when addressing a meeting on Clapham Common on Sunday night. It had been a long hard day and, with nothing going right in the Strike, he could be excused a little acerbity. Together with Haynes and Thiel he had been so much on the move since morning, trying to whip up flagging spirits by a series of speeches, all of them full of fire and optimism, and making the most of the promise of support and action that had reached them from sympathisers throughout the Labour movement their message was repetitious. The Police Union's fight was a fight for all.

In this respect the leadership's joint effort had received a welcome boost from a speaker who claimed to have received a telegram from the Triple Alliance, declaring a strike from midnight unless the Police Bill was withdrawn and the sacked policemen reinstated. A similar fighting spirit was shown by men from the rail unions – the NUR and ASLEF – and the delegates of the Licensed Vehicles Workers Union. All that NUPPO lacked, or so it seemed, was the support of its own members.

For hard though they strove to put a bold face on it, the lack of response to the strike by the rank and file of the Metropolitan force – traditionally the most militant of all – had badly shaken the NUPPO leaders, who now had the additional embarrassment of realising that, with the exception of Merseyside and Birmingham, the provincial branches had met the strike call with dismay and even hostility.

Earlier in the day, at yet another meeting on Tower Hill, the visiting delegates from Liverpool led by Halliday, had announced to wild applause that 1,600 of their comrades were out, nine out of every ten in the City Police. But reports since then had cast doubts on this assessment and, though this was not appreciated as yet, even stronger doubts were soon to be raised on the pledge from the Triple Alliance. Who sent the 'telegram'? Nobody was ever to know.

In these uncertain circumstances feelings were running high among the strikers about the men who remained on duty, some of whom – war veterans among them – were to receive from former mates a 'present' of white feathers.

'They will come out, or be forced out,' Hayes promised an audience in Croydon, while Marston's attack on the 'caterpillars' was still good enough to raise a cheer among the otherwise troubled assembly of the faithful at Clapham.

Ironically however – and even as Marston spoke – the 'caterpillars' of Liverpool were preparing to prove once more that, whatever other attributes they lacked, 'nerve' was not one of them. By Monday their courage – and the alchemists of Fleet Street – would have transformed the sluggish creatures into 'lions'.

Also on Monday the Press would be reporting, though more restrainedly, on yet another aspect of the city's drama: the death

157

of a looter, Cuthbert Howlett.

Heroism and homicide, each had a part to play. The stage was set for Liverpool's nastiest night.

CHAPTER ELEVEN

'To Glory We Steer!'

It was booze that killed Cuthbert Howlett. Booze and a soldier's bullet; a .303, fired from a Lee-Enfield.

As Corkhill sat contemplating the flames of 'anarchy' around him, and Marston turned 'caterpillar' into a word of shame, the city's crisis had claimed its fatal casualty – bestowing on Howlett a dubious immortality and getting the Sunday evening off to an ugly start.

The morning had begun peaceably enough, though the solemn call of the church bells had been accompanied by a noise less traditional to Liverpool's Sabbath: the sound of hammering as shopkeepers, all thought of holiday leisure now abandoned, boarded up their doors and empty windows, and tried to repair the damage of the night.

Traffic was light, the pavements almost deserted. Night rioters were notoriously late sleepers, and the police, completely exhausted, were content to sleep late as well. In the riot areas the armed sentries who had been posted to mount guard over the worst-hit premises, were the only concrete reminder of the army's presence.

It was not long, however, before the London Road began to recover from its hangover, as the first church-goers passed through on their way to early service. And, shortly afterwards, these were augmented by visitors from the suburbs: eager to establish that the rumours they had heard were true about the havoc wrought in the city centre . . .

Sightseers on a holiday jaunt to view the ruins; these were later to receive a rebuke from the Mayor, urging them to stay away for the sake of their personal safety; but, in the quiet of this

Sunday morning, such a warning would have seemed fanciful; besides, there was little else for them to do.

Down on the Pierhead, bills advertising Bank Holiday sailings to the Isle of Man had 'Cancelled' plastered across them. The ferries and their crews had been told to stay well clear. There were cancellations, too, of rail holiday traffic, ostensibly for the transport of further army units, but in reality because of the company's uncertainties over its staff. If the railwaymen lived up to their promises to the police strikers, there was the risk that stranded holidaymakers would vent their frustration on railway property.

Weighed against such problems of travel, and the dearth of traditional holiday entertainment, the 'ruins' had quite an attraction. Few of the visitors appeared to appreciate that by tomorrow there might be even bigger and better specimens on view.

It was not until lunchtime, when some of the leading characters of the previous night's entertainment began to drift into the pubs to meet together for their customary Sunday drinking, that the first signs appeared of the trouble to come.

With the drink flowing even faster than usual, and tongues being loosened accordingly, the events of the night before began to assume heroic dimensions for the less desirable patrons of the pubs that formed social centres for the depressed communities of the city. For others – better breeched than they – the rioting had been criminal conspiracy, a frightening insight into the horrors the breakdown of law could bring. But to the people of the rat-infested cottages that formed the worst of the city's festering slums, the crisis had been something very different, a chance to 'get even' with those above their station. An attempt at action, as distinct from their daily apathy, propping up street corners, and watching the world pass them by.

The police strikers had announced they were to hold yet another meeting, and march yet again to the Wellington Memorial. When this was over, so the rumour went, there would not be a serving scuffer in the city. They would *all* be on strike, every one of the old oppressors; and the sole defenders of the city would be soldiers, forbidden to shoot.

By the time the last round had been called, boasts of prowess in the law-breaking of the past had been replaced by glorious expectation of the future. Last night had been good despite the casualties. Tonight should prove infinitely better. In fact, the bully boys asked, why wait for night? Not a single copper stood between them and the loot of a lifetime. Not to mention a chance to slake their monumental thirst. So why not chance it now?

Among those advancing this attractive theme, with its emphasis on urgent and immediate self-help, the voice of Cuthbert Thomas Howlett was the loudest and most telling. A well-known figure to the CID, this small-time gang leader's aggressive stance and ready cunning had rapidly assured him a following among the locals, who habitually treated his suggestions with respect. Now, with his audience mulled out of their minds, and the pubs about to shut at any moment, this respect was replaced by drunken adulation.

Howlett's scheme for a breaking and entry daylight raid on certain premises off the Vauxhall Road, fringing the rear of the city's docks, made sense to all who knew their Merseyside geography. Here were the bottling stores and bonded warehouses, each of them offering an Aladdin's cave of treasure for the drinker and, because of that, in normal times placed under the close guardianship of the police. But now, with the cats away, was the time to play. Drink in glorious plenitude was the vision Howlett had shown them. And all of it looked like being theirs for the taking.

As the men left the pub behind them they were met by others – fellow victims of closing time – and their procession in its turn attracted the attention of still more. The crowd was a large one when it reached the first of its targets, a liquor bottling store, and had become a crazed mob when it reached the next.

So far Howlett's generalship had been exemplary. Everything had gone according to plan. Bottles by the crate-load had been sacrificed to the immediate thirst of the crowd. Hundreds more had been loaded for transit to 'safe places' and, hopefully, resale. It was not until they cracked open Burke's Bonded Warehouse in

161

neighbouring Love Lane, that they fell foul of the Sherwood Foresters.

The party was over. It had lasted far too long. Not content with their existing loot, and the damage they had inflicted while getting it, the gang and their mob followers had gone on to Burke's to drink more and destroy more as well. In fact this destruction appeared to have become their major object.

At their previous port of call they had smashed every bottle they could not empty or send away in the carts and barrows that had attached themselves to their tail. At Burke's it was even worse. Cask after cask was broken into and emptied, until the floor was awash with the spilled liquor: yet still the frenzied orgy continued, its participants reinforced by a continuous stream of new arrivals from the dock estate. Earlier, women had joined the menfolk in the drinking: at this stage they appeared to be leading them in the smashing. Their yells could be heard for streets away when the army arrived to put a stop to it.

As the two trucks pulled to a sudden halt, and the soldiers, in full battle order, jumped from the tailboards to rush the warehouse door, a woman screamed a warning to those around her to scatter and run. But some were too surprised to flee; even more were far too drunk to care.

A section of the Foresters made short work of these laggards, throwing them into the leading truck with a couple of sentries to guard them while the main detachment, under Second Lieutenant Jones, burst into the warehouse itself to tackle the rest of the rioters.

Here, however, they met with some resistance, and by the time they had managed to tow their prisoners to the trucks, the looters who had escaped the first rush had recovered their nerve, and the soldiers were treated to a shower of bricks and bottles.

But this, they later testified, was only a slight foretaste of the crisis that immediately followed.

Led by Howlett, and brandishing a variety of weapons – crowbars, sledgehammers, claw hammers among them – the crowd rushed in front of the leading truck and then surrounded it, clamouring for the release of the prisoners. A Sergeant fired warning shots into the air but this failed to impress the looters, fighting drunk as they were, and seconds later, they joined in a concerted charge.

Howlett, reaching for the side of the truck with one hand, and laying about him with a claw hammer with the other, was the first to reach the soldiers. Then, dropping the hammer he grabbed at a rifle held by Lance-Corporal Seymour and tried to wrest it from him. As he did so, the rest of the gang arrived and the Foresters, hopelessly outnumbered, struck back at them with rifle butts and bayonets.

It was a short, sharp, and madly mixed-up fight: its confusion to be reflected in the accounts of those who fought; each soldier seeing little more than his individual share of the action. But it seems certain that Seymour was quickly in difficulties in the tug of war over the rifle.

A lightweight compared with the hefty Howlett – fighting mad with the drink inside him – the Lance-Corporal was dragged towards the side of the truck. He was in danger of losing his balance and being pulled to the ground, but could not reach for support for fear of losing the rifle. 'There were five rounds of ammunition in that magazine,' he later testified, 'and I saw that if I was dragged off the five shots would be fired at the lorry.'

Instead, the bullets found Howlett.

The gang leader was taken to the Northern Hospital, where he died twelve hours later. The verdict of the Coroner's Court on Seymour's action was justifiable homicide.

The shots that killed Howlett had an immediate side-effect: a dramatic though temporary return to sobriety along the length of the Vauxhall Road. The crowd assaulting the truck had lost heart when their leader fell, and had dispersed shortly afterwards without any serious fighting. The soldiers, in their turn, contented themselves with making only a few arrests to add to the impressive bag already collected. Passions cooled down.

There was small sign, however, of any similar abatement in the political temperatures engendered by the Policemen's Strike, as was evident at a meeting called by the Liverpool Labour Party that same day. Probably one of the unkindest – and most wounding – cuts of all delivered to the Union and its leaders, had been the way in which old friends in Westminster had deserted the cause in its hour of trial. In Liverpool, Labour was made of sterner stuff.

'Speaking on behalf of the Labour Party,' Labour's readers in the Commons might well think fit to assure the House of 'their disapproval of a section of the Police in striking at a moment when efforts are being made to increase the liberty of the force.' But the views of these erstwhile 'comrades' were certainly not in harmony with those of Labour in the streets.

Almost on the eve of the strike, one of the party's most prominent trade union MPs, Mr C. W. Bowerman, had gone so far as to reflect that 'it is absurd to think that a Police Force can go on strike'.

Coming from a man who, until then, had been celebrated as one of the Union's most vocal champions, this revelation had shocked not only Marston and his colleagues, but the Liverpool Labour Party, determined at this Sabbath meeting to make amends.

Amid scenes of enthusiasm and emotion, the following resolution was approved: 'That Liverpool Trade Unionists declare common cause with the National Union of Police and Prison Officers and that, in order to give immediate and necessary assistance, a down tools policy be herewith declared.'

'All trade unionists of this district,' the resolution continued, 'are agreed to cease work at once.'

In Liverpool their hearts were indeed in the right place, and only those with a Westminster view of the public, and the value of good public relations, would have wondered about the location of their heads.

The first Police Strike had been popular with the voters. An affair they could understand, staged on a clear-out issue. Furthermore – even more important – it had been painless for the voter, and quickly over and done with. In 1919 the affair was complicated, and reactions extremely mixed.

The stroke of genius with which Macready, had persuaded the Home Office to make an immediate payment on account of the new pay scales, had demolished within a night the money grievances that had produced the big 'Yes' to the Union's Strike Questionnaire.

His firm warning to the Metropolitan Police of 30 May, imitated as it had been by the Provincial forces, had more than counterbalanced the Union's main weapon, threats of reprisals against those defying a strike call.

And the establishment of the Federation to represent all ranks of the police had not only served to undermine the very foundation of the Union, but had also confused the basic principles of the recognition issue.

Federation or Union? To most members of the public the choice had begun to appear, though erroneously, a narrow one. The skilful Government publicity over the remedying of the worst of the police grievances had caused the Union leaders to be increasingly, and unfairly, suspected of making their stand solely to maintain their own personal prestige.

Given such lack of enthusiasm among the community as a whole, the purges conducted in the Union Executive, and the complete rejection of the strike call by 95 per cent of the popular Metropolitan 'bobbies', the dearth of interest among the Party's national leadership for the militant action it had once appeared to support, seemed to many to be explicable, even inevitable.

The PR of the 'Prussian' Macready, the iron steadiness of Shortt, the ambivalences of the 'Wizard' in whom Marston had such trust . . . among them they had cut the ground beneath the Union's feet.

Even the Liverpool Labour leaders were to have second thoughts when they experienced the reaction of their members to the prospect of downing tools for 'bloody scuffers', and found themselves in danger of sharing the blame for the 'anarchy' the Strike had brought upon the city.

A state of anarchy? Tom O'Brien would not have known. Having come to his reluctant decision to back his friends by joining a strike he otherwise distrusted, he had stayed at home, as ordered by the Union, and as a result knew next to nothing of the threat hanging over the city.

Nor had the tone of the newspaper done much to enlighten him. In fact, to his mind, its denunciation of the strikers, coupled with dark hints of 'alien agitators' at work among the police, was so unbalanced as almost to support the NUPPO claim that the Press was part of an anti-trade union conspiracy.

Again, being published on Saturday morning – hours before the commencement of the major riots – the paper had little to report on the civic security aspect; incidents until then being relatively minor.

All the same, the day had found O'Brien in a restless and in-quisitive frame of mind. He was anxious for information about his comrades in the Liverpool force – was it true that some of them had declared against the Strike?

And he was also concerned about the response to the Strike call in forces outside the city: were they really coming out for the Union? And of course he wanted to know about the situation in his parish. Crown and Anchor schools would have a field day in the absence of the law.

Yet all he had heard to date had served only to confuse him. Fact and fiction were hard to separate. In later years a vivid pic-ture of what was happening in the embattled fringes of the city centre and the middle reaches of the Scotland Road would have been his for pressing the button of the television set. But in 1919, even the catwhisker (radio) was no more than a whisper in the ear of its inventor. Nor were there telephones for the homes of the humble PCs. He would just have to be patient.

By Sunday morning his patience had worn very thin. A mob running amok, within half a mile of the Garden? Looting and pil-lage in four districts throughout the night? The army taking over the city centre? Case-hardened to rumour begetting bigger rumours, he had dismissed at first what the neighbours told him as alarmist rubbish, but could the 'rubbish' have some basis in fact?

It was not in O'Brien's disposition – that of a policeman, and a good one at that – to be content for his information on the unchecked evidence of others. Nor was he prone to sit on his arse and do nothing when so much was reportedly happening in the streets outside. Yet, in effect, the Union had told him to do just that. He was to keep away from the police stations, except when on picket. He was to stay indoors, and wait for further instructions. So far he had not heard a damn word.

Having made his big decision and left the beat and gone home, O'Brien's first twinge of doubt had arisen over the rightness of the strike call, and even more, his quick response to it. While wholeheartedly applauding the objective, he had mistrusted the leadership's sense of timing. Suppose that events should prove the objective faulty too?

The doubt that had needled him then continued to needle him now. Had there really been so much trouble in the city, with him, Tom O'Brien, at home sleeping his head off, and leaving them to it? Had the Strike only served to tear the community apart? Momentarily, he was appalled at the thought of it, and the way he had put his family at risk for the sake of honour. Would 'honour' keep them fed while he waited in the work queue?

But then, to tilt the balance the other way, he remembered the tone of the Watch Committee's warning of dismissal – and all the old resentments came flooding back. How could a man when confronted by such arrogance do anything else but defy it? He had to give a short answer to those MPs who had dared to call the police strikers 'traitors'. It was intolerable to be described in such a context. A real provocation. For too long they had thought they owned the policemen body and soul: time, he resolved, to show them otherwise. So, as the day wore on, Tom O'Brien – 'a good copper' – continued to opt out of the unfamiliar drama, play with the kids and stay at home.

They could have done with Tom, and many another like him in the city that night. And, as the first murmurings of the mob began to be heard in the Scotland Road, 'Shiny' Salt was not the only one to think that the Watch Committee could have been more generous with their amnesty.

All sorts of characters caught up in the aftermath of the previous night's riots had been booked throughout the day, but the hard villains, the leaders who gave direction to the otherwise feckless mob had slipped through the net; there were too many holes in it. Nine hundred and fifty-five holes to be exact, or one for every fired policeman. The villains would be back in force tonight.

For Petchey, on duty in the relative peace and sanity of the Tue-brook there were similar reflections. Critical as ever of the NUPPO leadership for calling the strike, he was disgusted with the fashionable denigration of the strikers. The 'bolshevik' tag was rubbish, the 'traitor' label even worse. Many of the strikers were personal friends of his, and the very first to be appalled by the way in which their withdrawal had been seized upon by the mob. Many PCs would have been back in action like a shot – or so he reasoned – if it had not been too late.

The retirement, under orders, of the Tue-brook loyalists from their police station had proved to be only a temporary indignity, and they were now very much in business, though of an unspectacular sort.

Petchey himself was just completing a plain clothes assignment: watching the crowds as they left the pubs for old faces whose appearance could be a pointer to the location of the next bit of trouble to come. Also, he had helped tidy up the gambling-schools, and the gentlemen who ran them.

Misled by the unparalleled situation inside the city proper, where pitch and toss was being played openly within yards of Dale Street Police Station, these had imagined that the Police Strike's benefits applied to the Tue-brook district too. PC Petchey had disenchanted them.

But for all the quiet utility of his role and his liking for his parish and its people, Len Petchey felt that today he would rather be elsewhere: doing his stint in uniform, and nearer the front line. Up in the Scotland Road, and similar nests of rebellion, they would surely be needing all the help they could get.

'You have not heard of our flying column have you? No, because you are a respectable citizen. But the outlaws, the anarchists, the Bolsheviks who created a state of terrorism in Liverpool during the weekend know all about them. And the public of Liverpool have every reason to be proud and grateful to the men of our flying column, for it is they who have in the most part saved Liverpool.'

The *Liverpool Echo*'s revelations to its readers of the part that he and his comrades of the recruits' squad were playing in the defence of the city were received by Richard O'Keeffe with more than a grain of salt.

He had met, or collided with, battalions of unsavoury folk in the battle of the streets, but could not recall them telling him they were 'anarchists and bolsheviks': but then, of course, he had quite forgotten to ask. When clobbering a man who is attempting to clobber you, it's rare that you question his political affiliations.

All the same, and while making all the self-deprecatory gestures considered obligatory to Britons accused by the press of heroism, the men of the Squad were secretly very happy with the paper's praise. Until the riots they had been sensitive about the H numerals they carried on their shoulders, which marked them as probationers. Now they felt a tendency to flaunt them, though modestly of course.

The miseries of Saturday night, which did not seem too bad in retrospect, had been compounded during the day by visits from relatives and friends: these bringing the PCs the kit they had left behind when, so naively unaware of the events to come, they had last left 'home' for duty, early on Friday morning.

Soap, a towel, and best luxury of all – a razor! After he had bathed and shaved and applied the black Kiwi lavishly to toes and spine of his issue boots, young PC – but old soldier – O'Keeffe felt fit to take on the whole of the Scotland Road. When he said as much, however, the joke was poorly received. 'Maybe you'll need to,' replied the Station Sergeant.

The morale of the recruits had received yet a further boost from the provision of hot meals; well cooked, of large proportions, and a staggering innovation for the police canteens of frugal Liverpool. And then had followed a briefing in which they were informed not only of their role in the crisis, but also the form that the crisis was expected to take.

All normal working shifts for the daylight hours had been cancelled, and public order left to the army. Police resources were to be husbanded for the night, when both of the recruit squads could be hurled into the fight together. For a fight there would be: there was no conceivable doubt about that.

In their efforts to assess what their army allies would have called 'the strength and disposition of the enemy' – they could already guess his intentions! – the authorities had been severely handicapped by the absence of the uniformed patrols; normally their eyes and ears in times of trouble.

But it was known that loud boasts about a campaign of loot and pillage that would put that of the previous night to shame, were commonplace in every pub in the district.

And, even more ominously, it had been reported that the turbulent Irish off the Scotland Road had been observed erecting 'monuments'. Composed of huge piles of cobbles and paving stones these had been placed strategically on street corners throughout the area, where they could serve as ammunition against the intervention of the law.

Unwittingly, the Union's march through the city centre had also served to increase the confidence of the criminal community who were not to know that a good half of the 1,600 on parade were not police strikers but sympathisers, and thus conceived that ninety per cent of the force was 'OUT'.

In response to these and other indications of a worsening situation, and in the light of lessons learned the previous night, certain readjustments had been made in the city's security plans.

Instead of being held in reserve until called for, the army would be out in strength from the start. The soldiers would act simultaneously with the regular police in clearing the main thoroughfares of the crowds, while the CID and the specials would operate to their rear and on the flanks.

A favourite tactic with the rioters when confronted by opposition in force was to fall back, split up and take to the side

170

streets. There they would wait until the advance moved on, when they would re-emerge and return to the looting.

Now, however, it was planned that a mixed force of the CID and specials would follow behind the main advance, but at a considerable interval, so as to swoop on the enemy when he thought himself at his safest, catching him in a trap.

As an attempted solution to certain of the difficulties that had hampered operations the night before, the scheme had much to commend it, and was well received by its audience, though there was some surprise about the employment of the specials.

Hurriedly raised, without uniforms, and with only armbands to identify their status, the specials had been visualised as fulfilling a largely static role, such as safeguarding the banks and business houses where many of them were employed.

The fact that it had been considered necessary to use these untrained young men, most of them clerks and other white-collar workers from the suburbs, in the front line against the mob raised disturbing reflections on the numerical weakness of the police.

The CID's role as riot breaker also attracted the curiosity of the recruits. Until they had seen the detectives going into action in the London Road the previous night, they had assumed that they would be confined to operating in the intelligence field. But instead, the department which had ignored the strike call and remained loyal to a man, had been formed into a riot squad; very similar to their own.

Detachments of soldiers and regular policemen . . . of police recruits, CID and specials . . . some of the latter carrying pick handles as there were not enough truncheons to go round . . . it was a pretty variegated force that, on Sunday night, mustered for the defence of the city.

To the north, the Scotland Road had begun to boil, to the east the London Road was already boiling. Once more, as they marched through the uncannily empty streets of Liverpool 1 they heard in front of them the roar of a mindless mob.

It was afterwards said that when the news got around that the

Valiant was leaving the Fleet, and proceeding to the rescue of Liverpool, the Royal Marine band, aboard the flagship, struck up with 'Hearts of Oak'.

Apocryphal or not, the story was a neat comment on the attitude of the battleship's ship's company to the task ahead. 'Come, cheer up my lads, 'tis to glory we steer . . .'

So the army, the police force, and Uncle Tom Cobley and all, had got themselves into a spot and sent for Jolly Jack to bale them out! To the *Valiant*'s lower deck it was all rather hilarious. Their friends on holiday shore leave would have no idea of what they were missing.

The response of the Duty Commander at the Admiralty to the city's request for a battleship – 'Are you sure it's really necessary?' – had been echoed, with variations, along the chain of command, but as the ship left Scapa behind her, and turned her bows towards the south, the bridge at least was taking the matter seriously.

A signal was made to the escorting destroyers, *Venomous* and *Whitley*. They were to proceed ahead of her at maximum speed. The situation in Liverpool was getting beyond a joke.

CHAPTER TWELVE

Into the Cooler

The ingredients of the mob began to get together shortly after nine o'clock. Small groups of women at first, gossiping and laughing together as they waited for the start of the festivities to commence. Some had brought their children with them, kids who, barefoot often as not, contented themselves by playing among the lesser litter left from the night before, and since swept into the gutter by the shopkeepers, now absent.

The corner-boys were also assembling in quantity. Propping up the sooty walls with sagging shoulders, and extending their lean legs wearily across the paving stones, they eyed the scene expressionlessly and without comment to their neighbours: things would happen soon enough; they could leave the incentive to others. Occasionally, as he glanced at the peelers, drawn up in strength, one of them would remove the Woodie (cigarette) from his lips and, still expressionless, spit.

At the western end of the London Road, a thick, almost motionless, belt of navy-blue, dotted with shifting silver where buttons and helmet badges winked at each other beneath the new-lit street lights, the police stretched the breadth of the London Road, and were four lines deep. They had marched in from the city centre only a few moments earlier. Now, like the public, they waited.

The evening was oppressive, unhealthily sticky. The half-hearted breeze from the Mersey had collapsed in the city's dust. One of the sweating PCs, furtively unbuttoning the top of his uniform tunic, was pounced upon by a vigilant Sergeant and reprimanded. Strike or no, what remained of the city police force got small indulgence for lapses in petty discipline.

173

Behind the men were the approaches to the Plateau, its great buildings monuments to Liverpool's civic pride. And ahead of them was the memorial to a night of outrage, a cheerless vista, stretching to the right and left of the tramlines, of boarded-up doors and windows, empty and blacked-out shops.

The statistics of the damage in the London Road had only just come to hand. Over 200 premises had been broken into, and most of them stripped bare. A factory and distillery had been gutted, and plate glass destroyed by the acre. And all this had happened in a section that was less than 600 yards long.

When added to the toll exacted by the looters to the north, in the docks and along the Scotland Road, this was indeed a depressing return for the efforts of the army and the police, and cast a somewhat disparaging light on the earlier claims of 'victory'. Yet victory it had been, though limited in its scope. Things would have been worse – far worse – for the city, had its defenders broken: and every man of them knew it.

The baton charges, the snatch arrests, the punishment inflicted on the stone-throwers; these had not succeeded in preventing the destruction, but they certainly had contained it. Without them the mob would have been free to rampage through the city as a whole. Their job tonight was to hold the mob again.

It was ten o'clock when the crowds broke their murmuring expectancy and sprang noisily into life. Usually the violence started when it was time for the pubs to shut. And Sunday, 3 August, saw no departure from the norm.

As their menfolk, already inflamed by the bar-room talk of easy riches, plus the chance to give the upper crust a bloody nose, came out of the bars to further swell the crowds, the women rushed over to them, nagging them, embracing them, and some – the bolder ones – making derisive gestures to the police. These peelers alone stood between them and their shopping spree, blackleg peelers at that! Why wait any longer?

But it was not until a sudden massive flood of reinforcements reached it at the rear, that the crowd became a mob, and its movements a savage riot.

Although not everyone realised the fact, the new arrivals had tried their luck already on a less formidably guarded section of the road. No sooner had they got to work on a row of shops that had managed to survive their attentions of the night before, than they had been rudely interrupted by a strong detachment of infantry.

Charging from a side street with rifle butt and bayonet, the soldiers had taken the mob completely by surprise with the force of their violence. There was no warning, no parley, and even the toughest rioter had panicked and run. In a matter of minutes the street was clear.

But the army could not be everywhere at once, and the rioters who had fled the anger of the Tommies, quickly regrouped, moved westwards, and now were able to join the ranks of their brethren in confrontation with the police.

For a few minutes longer the uneasy lull persisted, and then, pushed by yet another swarm of trouble-makers to their rear, the front ranks went forward, their pace quickening to a run, and the whole mob surged towards the shops.

'I did my best to avoid my baton because it made such a sickening crunching sound when it collided with a human bone, but I did a fair amount of execution.'

Headlined, 'A Bobbie's Job', this description of the experiences of a special constable in Sunday's rioting, appeared in the *Liverpool Echo* the following Thursday, when the writer's apparent satisfaction at the damage he had helped inflict upon the rioters, attracted adverse criticism.

Appearing to prove that at least some members of the forces of law and order had actually enjoyed the opportunities for crunching heads that the crisis had afforded them, the letter aroused concern among those members of the public who had not experienced for themselves the ravages of the mob, or the extent of its ferocity.

'As you know,' the writer chattily continued, 'many of the police were in plain clothes. One energetic looter emerged from the crowd, and spoke to a police officer in plain clothes, taking him for a brother thief. He shouted "I've got a cash box. What have you got?" '

' "A baton," replied the PC, bringing it down on him.'

Few who had to cope with the looters on Sunday night would have shared the indignation showered upon the letter-writer, unfortunate though his breezy style might be. Richard O'Keeffe for one, had little time for recognising, let alone condemning, such nasty streaks as might be showing in the conduct of his colleagues. And as for himself, the motto was 'win or go under'.

The tone of recent briefings had left the PCs in no doubt that – in the current exceptional circumstances – it would be folly for them always to seek to conform to the rule book, and that blind eyes would be turned upon those breaching it. Goaded by the insults they had received and the spectacle of the damage, they needed little encouragement.

The best form of defence was attack and, even as the mob charged, so also did the police, using their truncheons with an effect that put their fiercest efforts of Saturday into the shade. And, to the PCs' aid came a long line of soldiers, anxious as they were – to quote one participant – 'to fix the buggers once and for all'.

This latter aim unfortunately proved to be premature, but the punishment meted out to the rioters was the severest yet. There was little or no attempt to take prisoners to add to the already overcrowded cells. The aim was to 'make an example', which they certainly succeeded in doing.

Not even when the rioters, leaving their worst casualties behind them, had fled into the side streets, did they find any breathing space from the law's pursuit. Already they had taken a beating from two of their enemies, the army and the uniformed police. Now they found themselves trapped in what had been their refuge by the enemy they hated most of all, the CID.

Although the magnificently built and heavy-handed uniformed 'scuffers' were respected and feared – though seldom loved – in the tough working-class districts of the Merseyside, the CID were hated with an almost pathological malevolence, a malevolence which in turn they often thoroughly reciprocated. The situation was so well-known that it was almost legendary.

To the average 'local' the PC on the beat was, though regrettably, part of the drear local landscape. Often he had served for years at one particular station, and had roots in the same indigent class as those around him. He could understand, though certainly not approve, the frustrations and enmities that rose from the grey world that shaped their lives: and sometimes, between the clouts he would even do you a good turn.

But the detective was, by nature of his job, a man from the outside, on brief and unrequested visits, looking in. A Peeping Tom on the district's unattractive nakedness, who then turned wholly contemptuous of the sins he saw.

Dirty bastards . . . scuffers in disguise . . . the CID men had a variety of titles, though very few were bold enough to quote them to their faces.

Given such circumstances, and the emotion-charged atmosphere of the moment, it says much for the city's need for information, and even more for the resolute calibre of the CID, that certain of its officers, regardless of the risks involved, operated throughout the disturbances in the heart of the rioters' territory.

Yet from the point of view of the authorities, the employment of the rest of their comrades in physical rough stuff against the rioters in the open, had an almost equally useful effect.

The shock felt by the rioters as, fleeing the London Road, they realised that these formidable old enemies were awaiting them, can be well imagined.

The plain clothes CID, by entering the back doubles from the rear had completely outwitted them at their own traditional game of hide and seek, and the penalties were heavy.

Before the fugitives had the slightest chance to recover, the detectives hurled themselves at them with fist and truncheon, and the riot became a rout. Such was the start of a series of bloody episodes where the 'dirty bastards' returned with interest the hate that the mob had bestowed on them.

'In considering the troubles in Liverpool a clear distinction must be made between the Police Strike and the hooliganism which it let loose. The strike was not the cause of the lawless outbreak but rather its opportunity. Yet reflective people see both point like fingerprints to anarchy . . .'

The Times was not alone in considering that certain sections of the Liverpool community were sub-human barbarians prepared to riot and destroy at any given opportunity. The city had been prone to violence and disorder from its birth.

In 1836, when it was recommended that Liverpool should scrap its antique Watch System and form a force modelled on the Metropolitan Police, founded seven years earlier, the Watch Committee disclosed that the city boasted no less than 2,000 'regularly practising thieves', as distinct from casuals, plus 600 'specialists' down at the docks. There were 'hundreds' of receivers of stolen property in the district, and 1,200 prostitutes within a fifteen-minute walk of Williamson Square, not far from the present-day police HQ in Hatton Garden.

Even when judged by the robust standards of the period, the thirst of the place was quite remarkable, with a quarter of the city's 1,600 pubs staying open after midnight.

Three-quarters of a century later that thirst was still unslaked, and destined, as so often in the past, to aggravate the city's instability.

'Anyone who knows the Scotland Road area understands its latest possibilities of riot and plunder,' the *Liverpool Echo* was to comment in the aftermath of the crisis. By then the recruits of the Flying Column had seen those 'possibilities' turned into hard fact.

The war in Liverpool had two major fronts. The London Road was one of them; the Scotland Road – 'Little Ireland' – was the other. When the police had been sent to their posts it had been touch and go as to which of these twin volcanoes would be the first to erupt.

In the event the London Road mob had led the field by an hour, but the Scotland Roaders, slow in starting, had certainly done their best to make up for the lost time.

Much of the loot from the liquor raids that had cost Howlett his life, had escaped the military, and finding its way into the district, had whetted the drinkers' appetite to go in search of more. And, with the aid of crowbar and jemmy, they were quick in finding it.

Originally the objective of the authorities had been to keep the disturbances confined to those areas that had been devastated during the previous rioting, but this proved impossible to realise.

With the bulk of the police and the army necessarily committed to the fighting in the London Road area, the resources were just not available for success on the second front. Soon the ravages of the riots in the north had engulfed not only the Scotland Road itself, but also Great Homer Street and Islington, and satellite streets around them.

Once more the law-abiding shuddered at the sound of cracking glass and the breaking down of doors. Following the events of the night before, certain prudent citizens had insured against disaster – or so they thought – by boarding up their shopfronts. To no avail. If anything, the sight of these precautions seemed to act as a stimulant to the wreckers, spurring them on to even greater effort. Shop after shop was entered and emptied. What could not be taken was destroyed.

Some of the women had brought empty prams and pushcarts to the scene to carry home their share of the pillage. For there was plenty for all and the mood of the rioters was generous.

At one point, a group of children were seen sitting on the kerb outside a shoe shop, breaking open cases of shoes and trying to match them with their feet. All that did not fit they hurled into the roadway.

Further on, having ransacked a furniture store, the mob had stacked together all the items that were too heavy to carry, and made a bonfire of the pile, dancing around it as it blazed.

Only in one of the jeweller's shops that they had made their major objectives, did the rioters meet their match. As a gang of them broke through the doorway the woman proprietor appeared at the top of the stairs, and blasted away at them with a revolver. Shots whining around their ears, they promptly bolted and after that the place was left well alone.

179

But, with this single exception, the mob was virtually unopposed. In the Scotland Road, Ritchie's hopeful appeal to the citizens to help organise their own defence had fallen on deaf ears.

Yet although this lack of spirit among the respectable burghers was to be roundly censured by the Mayor when later visiting the afflicted area – under heavy escort and in broad daylight – it had after all to be viewed against the size and temper of the mob.

'I am sorry this is late, I have had to defend myself with a revolver,' a Post Office employee scribbled on the back of a delayed telegram.

One of the very first incidents in the riot had arisen when roaming gangs stoned the late night tramcars, smashing their windows and forcing passengers into the street. On one end of the scales, even the shawlies were fair game for petty robbery. On the other, passing cars and carriages had been stopped and destroyed.

By midnight few of the inhabitants of the north side of the city would have quarrelled with Corkhill's claim of anarchy.

And, for the police and soldiers around the city centre, pausing briefly after their bloody victory in the London Road, a new front was opening, even more formidable than the old. As the tin-hatted Tommy in the leading truck of the convoy summed it up, 'Scotland Road. Here we come!'

As an example of bloody-minded destructiveness, the men of the Flying Column would have given full marks to the work of the mob in the London Road.

There was, for instance, the incident where a cash register, having been emptied of its contents, had been smashed with a hammer and then thrown through the plate glass window of a neighbouring shop. Talk about kicking a gift-horse in the teeth!

But the Scotland Road, littered with items pulled out of the shops just for the devil of it, was even more of an eye-opener. Already the troops had christened it 'The Occupied Territory'.

As they jumped from the trucks that had carried them through the district's perimeter, O'Keeffe and his comrade, John Ford, were astonished to be greeted by the sound of music: the latest ragtime hits being punched out on a piano.

Truncheons in fist they rounded the corner, startled figures flitting before them in the darkness, to be confronted by the spectacle of a grand piano along the kerbside with a host of drunken figures, men and women, beating out the time with mugs, bottles, and fists, and egging the pianist on.

The piano, sole survivor of many such in Cranes' music shop, had been dragged out of the window by the mob. The wreckage of the remainder had been pitched into the road.

'To make this Finnegan's Wake complete,' Ford later recorded, 'the place was strewn with beer bottles, yanked up from a broken-into bottling stores in Tariff Street, Vauxhall Road.'

As the police dashed forward the party broke up in disorder, but most of the revellers were too drunk to get away, and they, and a number of women found inside the premises, were promptly arrested.

A nearby bakery and a provision store had been plundered of their wares, and the women's aprons were full of edible loot. As the stuff slid from their pinnies the innocent looks on their faces seemed to Ford to border on the slapstick. 'Altogether it looked as if a good time was being had by all. And a pity perhaps to spoil it: but we did – and willingly.'

For probationary PCs O'Keeffe and Ford, the night had already been full of incident and surprise, but the surprises of Scotland Road beat the lot.

The mob, too, was to have its quota of shocks. First, and most unpleasant, being the arrival of the infantry and the squads of the Flying Column. Quite suddenly the street was full of fugitive figures streaming from their respected warrens in the looted shops, to form a shadowy mass retreating northwards, with the soldiers, their bayonets gleaming, pressing steadily in pursuit.

Nor, thanks to the new tactics agreed between the police and military commanders, did the mob's old and tried technique of scuttling into the side streets, and re-emerging later, have any luck.

When, after the line of soldiers had passed on, the rioters

milled out across the road again to continue with their interrupted plunder, the column swooped upon them from the rear.

It was familiar work then – the punch-up that followed – and
ended yet again in the triumph of the police.

When it was over, the backyards of the cottages and the lanes
behind them were carpeted with jettisoned loot . . .

Ladies' wear, mattresses, items of furniture, bales of cloth,
and above all, the booze . . . booze in great quantity . . . a magni-
ficent Bag!

But, as they surveyed with the aid of their bulls-eye lanterns
this treasure trove to which, unfortunately, they could stake no
claim, the recruits became aware that, although they might have
won another battle, they had not by a long chalk won the war.

From its northernmost point, its junction with the Blackstone
Boundary and Kirkdale Road, to its point of entry to the city
centre, a bare three hundred yards from Hatton Garden, the
Scotland Road stretched for over a mile. And, piercing its sides
from west and east were nearly forty secondary streets, with the
docklands on the one side, and Great Homer Street, its parallel,
on the other.

Even in the far more limited setting of the London Road the
security forces had found that the successful dispersal of a crowd
in one sector did not prevent a similar crowd from forming in
another. The police and military were too few in numbers to
cover every exit or entrance to the battlefield, and their success
in containing the excesses of the rioters had been obtained only
after the most exhausting manoeuvres; carried out 'at the
double', between the respective flashpoints.

In the Scotland Road the disabilities under which they
laboured were even worse. They were operating in the midst of a
community that, by reason of past history and present environ-
ment, was traditionally hostile, or at the best indifferent, to the
law and its enforcement. More, they were operating in an area
where the geography, as well as the numerical odds, were set
against them.

To contain a mob, however great its numbers, in the confines
of a district limited in its means of access was one thing. To do so

in circumstances where the mob would have available to it forty separate channels for reinforcement or retreat, was quite another.

Even as O'Keeffe and his comrades loaded their prisoners into the trucks that had followed up the advance, a huge influx of disorderly elements from the dock estate was pouring into the northern sectors of the road, while other gangs were reported on the prowl in the middle reaches of Great Homer Street. A little later came the news that the army had run into trouble.

As the soldiers continued their shoulder-to-shoulder advance up the Scotland Road the remnants of the crowd they had dispersed after the incident at Cranes had been joined by other fugitives. Bands of looters who had been busy in other shops, both in the road itself and the lesser streets around it, had taken fright on hearing of the arrival of the troops and police and brought with them a rumour that the soldiers had been ordered to shoot to kill.

Probably having its roots in the death of Cuthbert Howlett, the yarn produced a near-panic among its audience, and greatly accelerated its dispersal. But the dockers, who were next on the scene, were of tougher stuff and, having sampled some of the products of the O'Brien raid on the way, were in the mood for trouble. So, too, were the juvenile hooligans, whose preparations for it the day before had been noted by the CID.

As the soldiers moved along the main road, bathed in the light from the tall lamp standards, they were bombarded by hundreds of cobblestones and chunks of masonry hurled from the street intersections to their right. Meanwhile, taking fresh heart from this manifestation of support, and further encouraged by a reinforcement of shawlies and their menfolk who, cheated of earlier spoil, screamed to them to rush the shops and 'sweep the sojers aside', the rest of the rioters turned on their pursuers.

The situation was critical. The troops resentful and angry. There was live ammunition in their pouches. The mob was playing with fire.

As the stones continued to rain down upon his men, and the mob, with fresh recruits on its heels, started to press towards them, an officer loudly gave the order to load, followed almost immediately by the 'Present!'. But the yells and shouts of the mob, and its general intoxication, prevented the hint from registering, and the stones flew thicker than ever.

It was then that the order came to fire.

The volley, aimed over the heads of the 'enemy', echoed and re-echoed along the length of the road. To O'Keeffe, coming up with the police in support of the hard-pressed troops, it was just like old times.

But although they served to bring about a brief pause in its advance, bullets – when fired into the air – would not hold the mob for ever.

It was ten minutes or so later that the in-fighting began, following clashes between the army and the fringe of the crowd. It ended very quickly, after the troops had used their bayonets.

'It was the bayonets that did the trick,' O'Keeffe has since recalled. 'The soldiers' rush completely panicked the bully boys who fled in all directions. The points of the bayonets only were employed, but they were certainly effective. Many a rioter had a sore and bleeding posterior following that charge!'

Somewhat the worse for wear, and much the worse for temper, the security forces had won another battle: yet there were still more to come.

Once again the Riot Act was read: this time by the stipendiary magistrate outside the old Rotunda Theatre, at the top of the Scotland Road: and once again an armoured car was needed for the magistrate's protection against flying stones and bricks.

'It was the hottest night we'd had. There was incident after incident, and we charged with the baton, and the army with the bayonet, until we reached a stage where we felt we'd no breath left for any more and then, leaving the soldiers to settle things, we were rushed back to the London Road, where the old troubles had started up again.'

For O'Keeffe, one of the few brighter aspects of the night was exemplified by the appearance in court a few days later of a man charged with stealing jewellery from a looted jewellery shop. 'He asked for bail on the grounds that he had a bayonet wound in his back and the Stipendiary enquired, "You mean you're a wounded ex-soldier?"'

'Prisoner, "No, I was wounded in the London Road!"''

It was after 3 am before the streets were still again, and the PCs and the Tommies began their withdrawal to the city centre.

They had achieved, for all the ups and downs of the confused fighting that preceded it, a mastery over the city's crisis that they were never to lose.

And, rough though they had been in establishing that mastery, their very roughness had saved the rioters from something that would have been far worse.

They had succeeded in doing what many had privately feared would be impossible. They had saved a city, without recourse to a massacre. Only one man – Cuthbert Howlett – had died from a soldier's bullet. Only one man had been wounded by a bullet's ricochet.

In the Flying Column they were quite chuffed at the newspaper headlines, 'Police recruits and specials fight like lions!'

CHAPTER THIRTEEN

The Big Washout

'Central Liverpool tonight represents a war zone and as I write this evening the report comes in that there has been fighting, and wounds. . . . St George's Hall presides as an impressive background to a laager containing hundreds of soldiers. There are military lorries containing complements of armed men, awaiting any call that may be made, and, grimmest and most significant sight of all, several tanks.'

When *The Times* correspondent phoned his dispatch from the embattled city, the situation had reached its critical, and highly explosive, peak. A single spark, an angry finger on a trigger, a bayonet plunged too deeply . . . the consequences could have caused a chain reaction sufficient not only to overwhelm Liverpool itself, but also to shake every quarter of the country.

In such circumstances, reportage tended to be dramatic, and the headlines of the drama even more so. 'Cold Steel for Looters,' rejoiced the *Mirror* of Tuesday the 5th, telling its readers 'how the bayonet beat the hooligan mob.'

But, side by side with unstinting praise for the soldiers and the police, 'the men to whom the chief glory must go', was an increasingly vicious backlash of resentment aimed at the unlucky strikers, scapegoats for every horror the riots had produced.

Quick to anticipate this danger, the Union leaders had issued a strong denunciation of the riots and condemned the violence from which, as it pointed out, the Labour movement had everything to lose. But the *Liverpool Evening Echo* was not alone when it fulminated that:

'We see today that these policemen – they are now ex-policemen – who opened wide the floodgates which let in the mob are in haste to "condemn" the results of their own act. We see, too, that others who have associated themselves with the betrayers of the people also tumble over each other to "denounce" the very thing that was to be expected from the proceeding they support and approve for their own purposes.'

'People who play with fire,' the *Echo* continued, 'must accept the responsibility for what they do. After letting loose the mob deliberately and with open eyes, or after having approved or supported treason such as that, it is more than silly to "denounce" and to "condemn" what followed. It is unblushing impudence. It is adding insult to injury. They will not wash themselves clean in the public eyes so easily as that.'

In the letter columns of *The Times* righteousness triumphed over charity when readers gave their views on the culpability of the strikers; and a contribution from a person signing himself as 'Sacramentum' was fairly typical of the way the tide was flowing.

It appears from your columns that 800 men of the Metropolitan Force struck yesterday in violation of their oath of fealty. It is further stated that the men have been dismissed. In the course of a few days there will be agitation for the reinstatement of the deserters. The usual protests of victimisation will fill the sensitive ears of the House of Commons. But to yield to such solicitation would be fatal.

Every policeman is often called upon to give evidence on oath and his testimony that an accused person made to him when arrested and charged admission of guilt is commonly conclusive. Now these dismissed policemen are useless as witnesses. A short cross examination on the value they put on their oath and their regard for the law of the land would establish that they are not to be believed or trusted.

A similar line was taken in the House of Commons by Mr Rawlinson, KC, and, commenting on his speech, the *Echo* said: 'The foresworn must never be trusted again in the character of witnesses for the Crown.'

Although a cynic could have been forgiven for wondering why, if the oath was now so sacred to KCs and letter writers to *The Times*, not a dismissal had been made on that issue following the Strike of a year before; when well over 20,000 policemen had absented themselves from duty. Had Lloyd George's 'brilliant settlement' been accepted as absolution for their crime?

Apt or not, such critical reflections would have been ill-received by a public shocked by the extent of the riots and their implications. In the space of little more than three days, Society had been forced to reconsider the comforting assumptions of a lifetime, and would not likely forgive those who had made its disillusion possible. For decades it had nurtured its belief in the innate reasonableness and moderation of the British character and its inborn respect for law and order, and deep-rooted aversion to criminal and political violence. Yet, in just three days, one of the country's greatest cities had been occupied by a ravaging mob; the best part of that city's trusted 'bobbies' had gone on strike, and the army had been forced to open fire. The shock had been great; the urge for reprisals strong.

'Police who have departed from their pledge are nothing but liars.' So said Sir Leonard Dunning, Chief Inspector of Constabulary, attacking the strikers as having broken the oath. Such sweeping indictments were all too common.

But if Establishment reactions against the 'mutineers' were harsh and strong, equally so were the courts' reactions to the defeated rioters whom the 'loyalist' police were now bringing before them for judgment.

Sixty cases came before one magistrate alone that Bank Holiday Monday – all were remanded in custody for a week. By then the arrested totalled 350 plus nearly 100 more in Birkenhead. There were more to come.

At Birkenhead 53 people were charged on Monday with offences connected with the riots that had swept the town on Saturday and Sunday. There had been looting, attempted arson, and robberies with violence. Justice was swift and sharp, the objective seemingly that of avoiding long-drawn-out processes of trial in order to push the cases through the courts as soon as possible.

Most of the Birkenhead prisoners received two to three months in jail. One man, found with sixteen watches and forty rings in his possession was remanded in custody. So, too, was a gang of six men and two women who had been caught robbing a warehouse of £1,200 worth of whisky. The magistrates' statement that they intended to take 'the sternest measures against the prevailing spirit of lawlessness' proved to be no idle threat.

The Sergeant came up to the Squad, grinning all over his dial at sight of their unashamed fatigue as they staggered back into the Garden.

'Good work, lads. Bloody fine work. We'll be making bloody policemen of you yet.'

Policemen! To O'Keeffe the description sounded a little rich. If tangling with a mob in a short-range smashing match was all that police work was about then maybe the ex-Tommies of the squad could have taught the Sergeant a thing or two.

Wiping the sweat from his bruises, and with a brief moment in which to think, he was suddenly seized by the incongruity of it all.

Until now it had been action. Action all the way. Never a dull moment. But here, behind the massive Victorian brick of HQ — thick enough to stifle even the tanks' futile but thunderous parade — it was the action itself that had become unreal.

Was it minutes or hours since he, and the rest of the Squad, yelling the tribal war cries of the trenches, had plunged into fellow scouses as if they were bloody Jerries? The set-up confused him.

'Load. Present. Fire!' It was hard to realise that the commands had been screamed over a street that was only a penny tram ride from home. Or that the street lamps of Liverpool 5 had glittered on fixed bayonets?

The orderly atmosphere of the Garden banished his recollections. In his nostrils was the strong tang of floor polish and carbolic.

The last stages of the night's fight had been anything but clear cut. The soldiers had been left to the lion's share of breaking the resistance of the mob in the Scotland Road, but the police, when pulled back to settle the new outbreak in the London Road, had found the going tough.

In Christian Street, linking the two storm centres, they had been heavily stoned by hooligans who had positioned themselves to their front and flanks, and had to make repeated baton charges to clear the route. Then, back in the Road itself, they had found that, despite the punishment they had earlier dealt the mob, there were still sections of it determined to ask for more.

It had been – like Waterloo – a damn close run thing, but never once had the mob succeeded in breaking the thin blue line. And now the rain had come, hopefully to play the role of Marshal Blücher and save the day.

'Messy,' the Sergeant said, eyeing the jellied blood that clung to a squaddy's tunic, and making a whistling sound through his broad teeth as he thought about it. 'Bloody messy you could say!'

'But never mind,' he added after they had dutifully tittered at the joke, 'we'll soon get you another. There'll be plenty to replace it – from the strikers.'

The strikers. The poor bloody strikers. Surprisingly, a vague regret tempered the glow of self-satisfaction, and O'Keeffe was bone-weary.

With mumbled thanks to the volunteer helper, one of several who had come to lend a hand in the current emergency, he grabbed the enamel cup and gulped the rich sweet tea, downing it noisily with no pretext of politeness, and then, lowering himself on to the smooth polished comfortless lino, and propping his aching back and shoulders against the wall, he prepared to seek relief by slipping into a cat's nap of half dreams, with one ear cocked, of course, for further orders.

'London Road is the Ypres of Liverpool.' Quick to find an apt military simile to aid his explanation of the importance of the Flying Column's old battleground, *The Times'* correspondent also commented on the vast crowd of sightseers who had come into the city centre, a phenomenon that, running directly counter to their appeal for citizens to keep clear of the trouble areas, added to the multiple worries of Ritchie and Caldwell.

However, there were two sources of comfort available to the city fathers that had hitherto been lacking. One was the fact that it was continuing to rain; and rain heavily at that. Might not the weather quench the fire's smouldering embers?

But the other more material factor to encourage a mild optimism, was the arrival of the navy on Merseyside.

So far the requested battleship had not appeared. But the two destroyers that had steamed ahead of her were now moored alongside the Pierhead, and were preparing to land parties of blue-jackets to guard the docks.

More, far from bringing about the sort of confrontation that the Admiralty had feared, the arrival of the warships was proving popular with the locals. In fact, HMS *Venomous* and *Whitley* looked like becoming star attractions. Former rioters, it was said, were among the cheerful crowd who thronged the waterfront to welcome the two destroyers and their crews. Jolly Jack had again lived up to his role as a good ambassador; the fellow who could get away with things they would never forgive a soldier.

In the city itself things were beginning to look more settled. The crisis target figure of 2,000 special constables, to support the 250 specials normally attached to the force, had not only been reached but exceeded. The business community had been badly shaken by the knowledge that – had Ritchie's plea for self-help been met on the day he made it – much of the mob's damage to the London Road and Scotland Road would probably have been averted. Now, their lesson learnt, the banks, large stores and business houses had recalled employees from holidays to be organised for the defence of places where they worked.

When, on Monday morning, the massive grey silhouette of the battleship *Valiant* emerged from the rain haze, and nosed into the Mersey to drop anchor in mid-stream, Ritchie could at last begin to feel that things were beginning to look up. Not everyone would have agreed with him.

*   *   *

It might be Navy Week on the Mersey, but otherwise there were few attractions for Liverpudlians returning to the scarred city from their holiday break. Train traffic had been disrupted when some of the railwaymen, taking independent action, had come out in support of the Union.

The National Bakers' Strike, which had left shops throughout the country short of bread, had a predictably heavy impact on Liverpool where the mob had already devoured what stocks there were. And now the city had been afflicted by a tram drivers' strike.

Although this latter event, prosaically concerned with pay, was one that had no direct connection with the police dispute, Holliday, as NUPPO leader, had claimed publicly that it would be of great assistance to the Union, as a further example of the power of organised labour. At the time he was endeavouring to raise the spirits of an audience of strikers in London, but his word, played back, did little to endear him to his fellow citizens in the north.

But even though the strike's collapse in the Metropolitan force had saved them from the evils besetting Liverpool, Londoners, too, had their troubles as a result of the strikers' sympathisers; troubles reflected in traffic chaos at Waterloo.

At the start of the Bank Holiday, 500 engine drivers and firemen at the Great Western Railway Depot had pledged themselves to strike, and remain on strike 'until the Police Union is recognised and the Police Bill withdrawn.' Explained railwayman Tom Higgins, 'If the Government down the Police Union they will down us next.' The motormen of the City and South London tube railway were promising similar action for the morrow; tens of thousands of Londoners would have to walk to work.

Predictably Marston was to make the most of this brotherly support, hailing it as a token of the solidarity of the Labour Movement for the Union. But it was obvious that even the cancellation of the race train for Esher (Sandown Park) would scarcely be sufficient by itself to bring the Government to its knees.

Something more was needed – desperately needed – if

192

Macready's 'fiasco' jibe was not to be converted into fact.

In London, a few brave souls who had been on leave or sick at the Strike's commencement, had now returned to duty, and undeterred by the penalty had raised the total figure of those who had responded to the Union's call to 1,078. On the other side of the coin it was known, however, that very many of those who had come out with the first wave were regretting their action. Forty of them, mostly married men, had appealed to the Yard to be given a second chance and be taken back into the force as recruits. They had appealed in vain.

Nor was the picture of the strikers' morale any rosier in Birmingham where the turn out, originally claimed to be 400 with more to follow, had been revealed as 112. From the rest of the provincial police forces had come no response at all, except resolutions accusing the Union leadership of striking at the wrong time, in the wrong cause, and deceiving the membership about the Strike's general support.

Only a massive response from organised labour as a whole could prove the critics wrong. This the *Herald* bravely tried to supply.

In a leader deriding Macready and Shortt as being 'ostriches in their belief that the battle with the Union had been won', the *Herald* said,

> They announce it is a fiasco because they want it to be one. They hide their eyes and remark that they can see nothing happening. This is a complete miscalculation as to the principle involved and the force of the organised labour movement aroused in support of it. The Bill will be the first step towards depriving other powerful sections of *their* power – that is of the right of association. That is why other workers owe it to themselves to support the Police. That is why other workers are supporting them.

'That is why other workers are supporting them'. . . . It would take another quarter of a century and the ups and downs of yet another World War for 'wishful thinking' to become a phrase in general circulation: but the *Herald's* belief that labour would rally to NUPPO in its need provided a good example of the condition that phrase would describe.

The paper had published its leader knowing that the London Trades Council, the Liverpool Trades Council, various individual unions, and the TUC itself, had given, though in varying degree, their blessing to NUPPO and its cause.

More, the *Herald* could point out that only a month before, the national executive of the NUR had unanimously and publicly pledged support for the Police Union and that, currently, the south London motormen were showing by their sympathy strike that they at least believed their Executive had meant precisely what it said.

It was unfortunate for the newspaper that the apparently solid grounds on which it based its stand had the consistency of a quicksand – when subjected to the flexible ideas of Jim Thomas.

First hint of the blow that was to destroy the NUPPO leadership's one hope of survival – the involvement of other unions in their fight – came when the erstwhile genial and chummy 'Jimmy', then General Secretary of the NUR, stated ominously, 'I am submitting the whole matter of the railwaymen's attitude in connection with the police dispute to the Executive Committee tomorrow. The action of certain men in already striking is not only a grave mistake, but one for which the Union is not, and cannot be, in any way responsible.'

Under no consideration, he added, 'should members be influenced by local circumstances, passion or prejudice.' They should go on with their work until they received instructions from their Executives.

The blow itself struck home the following day, delivered by the NUR Executive in a terse statement that concluded, 'The best interests of the railwaymen will be served by those on strike returning to work.'

It was the beginning of the end.

'Not a wheel will turn. Not a train will run . . .'. The dramatic phrase, and his doubts about its validity when he had heard it flung at the crowd at that packed meeting in the Stadium, came back vividly to Leonard Petchey as he opened his newspaper and read the headlines 'Disillusioned railwaymen see the light.'

So much, then, for the resolutions, the manifestos, the delegates' applause! Petchey was not unduly surprised that, when it came to testing time the NUR should have put the best interests of its own members before those of the Police Union: *that*, after all, was what they were elected to do. But what did surprise him was that the NUR apologia should have been so coldly phrased. 'After all that had been said, all the promises that had been made, there was not even a word of sympathy for the people they'd once called their brothers.'

To this day, Leonard Petchey, though so much out of sympathy with the Strike and its leaders, can remember his disgusted reaction to the 'callous' treatment afforded them by their former allies.

However, it is probable that Petchey's notable fellow loyalist – Major-General Sir Nevil Macready – would have considered the PC's reaction to have been a little naïve.

The Commissioner had never shared the fears of weaker colleagues that a head-on collision with NUPPO would be the signal for a showdown with the embattled might of the Triple Alliance. Eloquent words were one thing, when employed in a popular cause, but the NUPPO cause was no longer sufficiently viable for it to justify a call for socialist martyrs.

'Organised labour' had given its pledges to a union whose leaders appeared to have the overwhelming backing of its members, and a massive mandate for strike action, confirmed by ballot. But NUPPO today was a vastly different proposition. It was split right down the seam. And he, Macready, had done quite a bit of the splitting.

The Government's promise to introduce the improvements in pay and conditions suggested by Desborough, and its prompt payment of a lump sum in token of goodwill, had isolated the leadership from the rank and file, who were then ordered to strike – and incur the dismissal penalty – for what appeared to be the supremacy of the Union alone.

So how could Thomas approve a strike by NUR members in sympathy with a Union, the bulk of whose members worked on? And what credit could Thomas – and the Labour Movement – hope to gain from backing a cause that so obviously was unpopular with the public? To the Commissioner who knew an aspiring politician when he saw one, it was just not on. Thomas had shifted the ground from beneath the militants' feet.

Understandably, in the years to come, PCs whose careers had been ruined by the failure of the Strike, were to place considerable blame on the Labour Movement for having misled them over the support it would afford strike action.

But 'deception' could also be laid to the charge of the NUPPO leaders, according to the Commissioner's memoirs, for he records that, following the Thomas 'betrayal',

> The head of the Battersea branch of the National Union of Railwaymen, a certain Mr Oliver, had called his men out in sympathy with the Police Union, and finding that he was not supported by his own union was in an uncomfortable position. He came to see me with the idea that if he could persuade me to reinstate the dismissed men he would be able to retire gracefully from the awkward position he had got himself into. He acknowledged that he had been misled by the false reports spread by Hayes and the union, who told him that 5,000 police were out on the 3rd of August . . .

Hayes, should the account be correct, had exaggerated the true figure by five hundred per cent.

Whatever the rights and wrongs of the NUR's about-turn in the police crisis, the *Herald* had not been alone in miscalculating the extent of working-class support for the Police Union's showdown with what now had become the Law. No less a Labour personality than Tom Mann had shared the newspaper's fatal delusion.

Mann's arrival on the Liverpool scene on Tuesday had brought fresh hope to the discouraged strikers and renewed nervousness among the city's conservative element. It also brought out a show of trade union solidarity that caused the authorities to bar the Plateau to marchers and demonstrators, and led to an eyeball to eyeball confrontation between troops and unionists outside St George's Hall.

It was a moment that brought back to Salt and Petchey, and conceivably to the labour veterans too, black memories of that day in 1911 when police and army intervention against a similar visit had brought death and injury to a rally that had turned into a riot: but this time Mann's message was to 'let byegones be byegones' and the affair passed off peaceably, though in an atmosphere of tension.

Experienced the hard way through decades of industrial conflict, Mann's first concern was to obtain renewal of the promises given the strikers by local Union officials, and to appoint a Strike Committee.

Delegates were also nominated to interview the Watch Committees of Liverpool, Birkenhead, Wallasey, and Bootle.

They would demand not only the reinstatement of the policemen on strike, but also the full recognition of the right of the police to form a trade union.

Then, following a late night meeting with his colleagues, he stated, 'I am satisfied the whole thing is well in hand. Optimism prevails. Victory is certain.'

It was a miscalculation that made the *Herald's* pale into insignificance.

Measured against the furious conflicts that had raged through the streets during the weekend, Tuesday and Wednesday were relatively quiet. But they still held enough mischief to keep the police gainfully employed. And would continue to do so for at least a week to come.

Due to an influx of reinforcements from the services, the riots had been reduced to skirmishes and slowly the authorities had begun to switch from the defensive. House to house searches had already been instituted, and each doorway saw the recovery of loot taken by the rioters and a fresh tally of arrests and sentences.

For the recruits of the Column, life was certainly a lot easier, even though they were still not permitted to go home. 'Sleeping accommodation had been provided in Lincoln Lodge, in bunk beds once used by USA personnel awaiting return to America.' But otherwise the Garden, to which they were marched at 6 am each day, remained their *pied-à-terre*.

It was an odd sort of routine with the spit and polish tradition for which the Liverpool force had been noted, waived temporarily for an emergency that might require them at one moment to engage hand to hand with a gang of looters, and at another to search through piles of stinking garbage, camouflage for a cache of stolen property.

All the same the routine had its compensations, some of them quite unexpected. To the astonishment of veterans of the force, accustomed to its severities of discipline, and its tradition of isolation from the social life of the city, both the authorities and the general public were quick to show appreciation of their work.

Concerts were provided for the men during their enforced stay at the Garden, and on one occasion the full orchestra from Lyons' State Cafe came along and played for them. 'It must have been a long time, if ever,' O'Keeffe said later, 'that the old parade-room let its hair down and went all arty arty!'

In fact there was only one thing to mar the recruits' (temporary) contentment with their lot, and that was the sight of the pile of uniforms, daily growing higher, as sometimes individually, and sometimes in groups, the men who once had worn them obeyed the last order the force was ever to give them, and handed them back.

CHAPTER FOURTEEN

Aftermath

Inside Liverpool's Rose Hill police station the shapeless mound of discarded dark blue uniforms and helmets was growing larger every hour.

To O'Keeffe, sent there to solace some marooned detectives with a couple of army dixies of 'Scouse', it was even more impressive, and more poignant than the similar mound in the Garden.

Several of the cast-off tunics carried the bright splash of medal ribbons. Long Service. Good Conduct. Personal Gallantry. 'But none of them much cop now,' said someone idly, quite unconscious of the pun. Rose Hill was no place for the light-hearted: not just now.

There were other ribbons, too, on the breasts of the uniforms, mementoes of times when the men, so recently dismissed as 'mutineers', had been hailed as heroes for services, performed in scarlet and khaki in the Empire's cause.

In the War in the Sudan, the War in South Africa, the War in Europe, only recently concluded, Liverpool policemen had extended the horizon of their beats to the Himalayan passes and the veldt of the Transvaal. But now, like the careers and livelihood of those who had proudly worn them, tunics and ribbons lay ingloriously in the dust.

'What a waste,' O'Keeffe thought frantically. 'What a bloody terrible waste!'

But he did not know whether he was at liberty to say it. Not when the sacked men were veterans, and he just a raw recruit.

Spruce yet oddly constrained in unfamiliar civvies, as though reluctantly encased in somebody else's clothes, yet another of the

199

dismissed men had come into the hallway from Peover Street to add his contribution to the mound.

'Old enough to be my Dad,' he noted grimly, exasperation and pity grabbing him by the throat.

But the new arrival did not dump his uniform as some of the militants had done who had come before him, expressing as they did so their anger and contempt. Nor did he hesitate as others had hesitated – sheepish as though for the first time aware of what they had done, and the gravity of its consequences.

Instead, thumbing tunic and trousers with measured care, as if to ensure their creases were set in true, to conform with regulations, he laid them down solemnly, with a sort of mournful reverence; a veteran placing a wreath before a cenotaph.

The buttons had been newly polished, and they showed it. On the well brushed sleeve glinted three silver stripes.

'So you're one of the city's heroes?' he queried, spotting the silent O'Keeffe. 'One of the lads who signed on at the start of it all!'

And then, without waiting for the recruit's embarrassed answer, but merely gesturing to the tell-tale heap, he added in a voice devoid of malice: 'It meant a lot to me once, the stuff you see in front of you. Maybe it will mean a lot to you as well. So just take a tip from an old hand if it does and don't fly against the rules. They'll beat you in the end, whatever the quarrel may be.'

There was silence for a moment, before he concluded: 'But don't expect a thank you, whatever you may do. Just use your loaf lad, and keep out of bleeding trouble!'

And at that, the Sergeant that-had-been turned smartly on his heel, and without a backward glance, walked out into the riot-scarred streets, and the uncertainties of the future.

'What a bloody waste. What a bloody terrible waste!' But this time O'Keeffe expressed his thoughts aloud.

Tom Milburn (ex-PC 97) handed in his uniform at Prescot Street. The old place was so full of new faces – faces he had never seen before – that he felt a stranger to it.

These new recruits were not the squaddies of the Flying

Column but men who had joined only a day or two before in reply to an advertisement by the Watch Committee for replacements for the dismissed strikers.

Most of them were ex-soldiers, only recently demobbed, and their presence gave rise to further reflections on the wisdom of Hayes and Marston in calling the Strike when they did.

From the very first it had been argued that, even disregarding the effect of the new concessions on the broad mass of the membership, the time was not nearly so favourable for strike action as it had been the year before.

The country was then at war, and desperately short of manpower. But now the armies were rapidly being run down, the munitions factories were closing, literally hundreds of thousands of men were seeking work.

The Watch Committee had advertised on the Saturday. The depleted ranks of the City Police Force had been filled in less than a week.

'So it's goodbye then?' At last Milburn saw someone he knew, a former comrade, but now a loyalist. There were no hard feelings: just a bit of mutual embarassment. Briefly the two men shook hands, and wished each other good luck, and then, pressing his way through the unfamiliar throng, Milburn was down the station steps and on to the street again, and going home to his wife and the two children, under five.

Ahead of him, though he did not know it yet, was a job on a farm, completely unfamiliar to a copper who had had his beat in Liverpool 5 – 'but my wife was a good manager, and we were able to cope, thank God.'

To Tom O'Brien the order that police strikers must forthwith return their uniforms came as no surprise; all the same, he felt, they could have dispensed with the dig that went with it.

'Where police who have been on strike and have been dismissed neglect to return their uniforms warrants will be issued for their recovery. Civilians must not possess them.'

Did they think the 'civilians' would hock them? Or use them as camouflage for crime? 'We're not all *that* hard-up,' he reflected wryly, adding as proviso, however, 'at least not YET.'

O'Brien, like Milburn, had no hard feelings as he handed in his gear. These would arise later when, in its most imperious pre-Strike style, authority would issue the order that no former striker would be allowed on police premises, and his wife had to go and collect the week's pay that was due to him.

Even Tom Mann could not hope to pull out organised labour now. Chastened by the NUR's decree, the Liverpool railwaymen, hitherto distinguished as NUPPO's most vocal supporters, decided they had no choice but to comply, though adding to their resolution a face-saver to the effect that they continued to 'demand' the men's reinstatement.

The municipal workers, too, had been ordered to stay aloof, and the dockers had turned down the idea of a strike to save the scuffers: old memories died hard. The Triple Alliance had axes of its own to grind. It would strike, if it struck at all, in its own cause and no other.

Nor did the Labour leader have any better luck in his approaches to the civic authorities. When 'The Police Dispute Negotiating Committee' – largely Mann's own brainchild – demanded 'the urgent withdrawal of notices and return of uniforms' (to their former wearers) authority did not even deign to reply. The planned representations to the Merseyside Watch Committees also came to nothing: Caldwell, setting the pace in Liverpool for Birkenhead and Bootle to follow, arguing that he had no power to arrange such an early meeting.

Bravely, the Committee did its best to cover its ill-success to date by portentous hints of the power at its disposal for the future. If its demands were not met, said a Committee spokesman, 'nearly all' the Lancashire Borough forces would come out on strike.

Its demands were not met. The Borough forces predictably stayed put.

It was on Saturday the 9th that the recriminations began. The strike was then eight days old, but to many it might have been so many years: so much had changed, and so much more was changing.

And among those changes one of the most striking was the relationship, hitherto so close, between the leaders of the Police Union and those of the trade union movement as a whole.

It was the *Herald* that dared bring the issue to the surface in a blistering editorial that recalled,

> Months ago the Police Union was admitted to membership of the National Labour Party; it was affiliated to the Trade Union Congress, and, as a Trade Union, was invited to take part, and did take part, in the Industrial Conference summoned by the Government itself to discuss and formulate schemes for averting industrial trouble.
>
> Many Trade Union branches, many Trade Union executives, pledged themselves to support the Police in maintaining their position. And yet, with the exception of a sectional strike or so, nowhere has any real backing been given to the Police, save from Liverpool.

And the *Herald* then emphasised:

> We want very strongly indeed to point out the gross injustice and disloyalty to their comrades which is involved when branches of trade unions and executives pass resolutions pledging support and then fail to give it. We do not propose — it is not our business — to apportion the blame. The whole movement must share in whatever odium attaches to it for having failed to carry out the pledges and promises made to the Police.

Even Tom Mann found it necessary to stress, in an appeal to Labour issued on the same day as the *Herald*'s strictures, 'I write to inform all who care for my opinion that unless we do now take this matter seriously in hand, and refuse to allow the police to be deprived of their right to have a trade union, we shall be guilty of gross breach of faith with the police. Comrades of the port of Liverpool, the time for straight-out action has arrived.'

But what of the views of the NUPPO leaders themselves, the

men who, in the period running up to the Strike declaration, had so often boasted of the might of the Labour Movement being solidly behind them?

Always with one eye attentive to the sensitivities of missing allies, and the party of which he was to become a prominent member, Hayes preferred to concentrate his attack on the NUPPO membership, for failing to respond to the Strike call.

Speaking at a Hyde Park rally, he recalled that only two months before, 44,000 policemen and members of the prison service had been in favour of strike action, yet only 'about 5,000' were out. This, said Hayes, 'showed that the grasping spirit was stronger than principle.'

His critics would later argue that the '5,000' figure showed that Hayes's desire to impress was stronger than his arithmetic.

It was left to the radical Jim Marston to be tactless enough to revert to Labour's role in what Macready had described as the 'fiasco'.

'The fact that the Government is taking away from the Police the right of organising will react on every working man,' he claimed, and then recalled that, before the crisis, 'Labour pledged itself all over the country to support the Police. In every Labour institute throughout England, fierce resolutions were passed saying that they were out to go to the full length. Their failure to do so is not the fault of the majority of the organised workers.' He implied that it was the leadership of the unions that should bear the blame.

On Sunday the 10th a mass meeting of sympathisers in Hyde Park called for 'all trade unions to down tools in the event of the non-withdrawal of the Police Bill and the reinstatement of all strikers.' Resolutions were also passed calling for Shortt's resignation, and Macready's dismissal. It must have seemed to the increasingly lonely NUPPO strikers a warming echo of old times.

The same day Macready announced laconically that the emergency was over, and that members of the Metropolitan force could resume normal leave.

Normal leave? It might be all right for the Metropolis, but in

Liverpool it seemed as remote as ever. The riots were over, but 'incidents' abounded. For O'Keeffe, John Ford, Leonard Petchey *et al* the days were crowded, and the nights extremely noisy.

On the Thursday, militant members of the National Federation of Discharged Soldiers clashed with army men guarding the Plateau. One of the demonstrators, William McGinty, tried to wrest a rifle from an isolated sentry and the troops charged with the bayonet. McGinty was subsequently sentenced to a month's imprisonment.

Meanwhile, to cope with isolated cases of looting, two armoured cars were added to the army's resources in the city.

'In all cities,' said Mr Justice Avory commenting on the consequences of the Police strike on Merseyside, 'there is a certain class of people who are only kept in restraint by the presence of the police force, and who are ready at a moment's notice to take advantage of the absence of the policeman from his beat . . .'

In Liverpool, what had originally been viewed as a confrontation between the members of the police force and the police authorities had resulted in something that very few, on either side, had bargained for; and even fewer had found welcome: an attempt at mob rule. And, for the mob's attempt, the striking police paid dear.

At a Watch Committee meeting of 23 August 1919, letters were read regarding the strikers. Mrs Louise Hughes, Acting Secretary, Liverpool Women's Citizens Association, wrote on behalf of that organisation asking that efforts should be made to find the strikers employment to prevent their families suffering.

In far less charitable vein, a letter from the Mossley Hill Conservative and Unionist Club forwarded a resolution that read: 'We unanimously protest against paying any increased taxation due to the mob outrage, if any of the strikers are reinstated.'

Somewhat belatedly, some of the Labour members of the Council attempted to secure reinstatement for the sacked men, at a council meeting held on 3 September.

It was proposed by Councillor Robinson, and seconded by Councillor Keene, 'that this Council, while regretting the action which culminated in the recent police strike, desires in consequence of their long and faithful service (both civil and military) to recommend to the Watch Committee the advisability of reinstating the men.'

The resolution was defeated by 65 votes to 25.

Earlier, a deputation from the Parliamentary Committee of the Trades Union Congress, also pressing for reinstatement had been told by Edward Shortt: 'This can not possibly be done. Notice was given as far back as last May that in the event of any men absenting themselves without reasonable cause they would be instantly dismissed with forfeiture of pension rights.'

Yet behind this apparently clear-cut and foregone conclusion of the Home Office, duplicated by the Watch Committee of every authority affected by the strike, was much that today can be classed as obscure, and even bewildering.

In Liverpool this is particularly so: one of the strangest features being that there is no direct mention whatsoever of the Strike in the Head Constable's Reports that Caldwell submitted to the Watch Committee. Nor indeed is there such mention in the published proceedings of the Watch Committee itself.

Instead, the Head Constable's Report Book for the week ending 8 August 1919 merely states: '955 strikers dismissed.' And the report is unsigned.

'The manner in which the strikers were dismissed,' says Douglas Massey, in a thesis on the Strike written for the Ethel Wormald College of Education, 'has an air of mystery about it.'

And he goes on to point out that in the Punishment Book, in which dismissals are recorded, there is no counter-entry against the Head Constable's (unsigned) report.

'More, it would seem that neither then nor since has anyone thought of questioning the legality of the summary dismissal of the men, all of whom were serving officers working under a discipline code which laid down procedure with regard to the manner in which they could be punished.'

In fact, however, none of the strikers were given the opportunity to defend themselves, but simply informed that they had been dismissed. And, incredibly – by the standards of our day –

they would appear to have accepted that dismissal without any challenge in the courts.

The Strike born in confusion had died in confusion. Its major victims, the strikers, being sacrificed as an example to the future.

> You stick to the Police, lads!
> You save your lives;
> You have something to keep, lads!
> You have your children and wives!
> If you go on strike, my boys,
> You will get no pay
> So think of your wives and kids, lads
> And stick to old Macey . . .

There will always be someone willing to laugh at a passing funeral, and the poet who contributed 'The Song of the H Division Police' ('to be sung in the canteen to the tune of "The Red Flag"') must have been an excellent example of the breed. 'The literary merit of the effort is not strong,' the Editor of the *East London Observer* was forced to concede, 'but the sentiment is admirable.'

The humour was inspired by the fact that it had been reported that, of the 128 officers and men in H – Whitechapel – Division, only 8 had gone on strike, and none, so it seemed, in neighbouring Limehouse. But it is probable that the errant eight's own unique sense of humour made more appeal to their fellow cockneys, watching them parade in their Sunday best, to return their uniforms in style: in a coster's barrow.

Mooching amid these other blue mounds up in Liverpool's Rose Hill, O'Keeffe found some old fashioned bulls-eye lanterns, and decided to take one, as a souvenir. He also retrieved an old and shiny notebook cover from the same collection, and retained it till the end of his service. Many a time in the years to come was he to ponder on the identity of its previous owner. A good copper, he was sure of it, and, but for the grace of God, it could have been him.

Conclusion

During the course of the Police Strike of 1919 the newspapers carried much that would make familiar reading today.

The *Daily Mirror*, alarmed by the rate of inflation, was urging a policy of wage restraint, arguing that trade unionists should worry less about increasing the size of their pay packets and more about spiralling prices.

In *The Times* there were reflections on the race riots in Chicago, in which nearly fifty people had been killed.

There was trouble in the coal industry, 'terrorism' in Ireland, and concern among ecclesiastics about the sufferings of what is now called The Third World, in particular the starving millions of Asia Minor.

Engine drivers were threatening a national rail strike. The bakers were staging a baker's strike. And 'direct action' – the use of the strike weapon for purely political ends – was being urged upon the unions as means of ending Britain's intervention against the Bolsheviks in Russia.

'There used to be a tantalising game of puppets,' said the *Mirror*. 'A mechanical device in which you knocked down one wooden figure only to see another pop up. The puzzle was to keep all the figures flat at the same moment. Our strikes have the same habit of perpetual recrudescence. We settle, or hope to settle, or appear to settle one. Immediately another appears on the horizon. It was (and still is) coal. It is the police. It is, or maybe, the bakers. What will it be tomorrow?'

And, in the same issue that announced 'Surprise Police Strike', a doom-laden reader commented: 'It is certain that in the end the whole world will again revert to savagery. We have climbed from the depths of barbarism to the highest pinnacle of civilisation and now, in accordance with the laws of nature, we must begin to descend. The last state of the world will be the same as the first – dense forests, gigantic animals and savage men.'

In October 1969, a half century after that gloomy forecast the policemen of Montreal – demanding an £800 increase on their minimum wage of £3,000 – decided to follow the example of their British colleagues, and went on strike.

Within hours three people had been shot dead, ten bank hold-ups had been staged, four hotels had been 'invaded' and wrecked, thirty-five businesses and scores of shops had been looted, hundreds of people had been injured in trying to protect their property, and a full-scale gun battle was raging around the HQ of a bus company, besieged by taxi-men protesting at its monopoly of traffic from the airport.

By nightfall the skies were red with the flames of arson. Gangs of youths, armed with hatchets, and shouting the Marxist separatist slogan of 'Quebecois dans les rues', were battering cars to pieces and beating up their occupants.

Provincial police sent to the city were disarmed, their patrol cars overturned and set on fire. Army detachments, supported by Mounties, had to protect the Town Hall and the massive television-radio tower.

And only after the Quebec Government had rushed an emergency Bill through the National Assembly which threatened the strikers with jail, or a £40 fine for each day they stayed off duty, did the police return to their posts and bring the riot under control.

The police strike had lasted only fifteen hours, yet had cost this prosperous city, with a population less than a quarter that of London, more than a million pounds worth of damage, and had kept tens of thousands of its citizens confined to their homes, in a state of terror.

'Had the police stayed out another day,' said one of these Montrealers, 'there would have been a massacre. The rioters were like madmen, or wild animals. They threw Molotov cocktails through doors and windows, knowing that the fire service had come out in support of the police. They caught four young provincial policemen down our way and trampled them underfoot. It shocked us all, this revelation of the extent of the violence that lay beneath the surface and how quickly normality could snap, and be replaced by nightmare.'

The Police Strike of 1919 involved slightly less than three per cent of the total police strength throughout the country. Even in Liverpool, nearly half of the City Police force stayed loyal. Yet the rioting was serious enough to literally shock the nation and cause it, though for all too brief a period, to examine its conscience regarding the way in which it had taken its 'bobbies' for granted.

For the first time in the modern era the authorities had lost control, and the mob had taken charge in a British city. Would it also be the last time, or was this just a taste of things to come? If the police had struck in greater numbers, and struck in all the other large cities too, what then would have happened to our 'tolerant' society?

At the time, the point was repeatedly made that Liverpool, by reason of its embittered industrial history and its mixture of communities and loyalties, was a special case, and unrepresentative of the country as a whole. Can the same be said in the circumstances that prevail in our cities today?

A soaring crime rate, in which murder and rape are everyday occurrences, a social climate in which confrontation thrives as never before and in which violence has become regarded as a legitimate political weapon, augurs ill for complacency.

In the end we will get the police force – or the crime wave – we deserve.

'Put brutally', as a senior police officer recently said to me. 'It's a question of choice.'

Index

Index

212

Index

McGinty, William 205
Macready, Charles 13
Macready, Lieutenant General Sir Nevil 13, 14, 15, 18–20, 22–55, 61–66, 68, 71, 83, 85–88, 90–93, 104, 108, 109, 122, 128, 129, 165, 193, 195, 196, 204
Manchester 40, 53
Mann, Thomas 59–61, 196, 202, 203
Marshall, Paddy 132, 133
Marston, PC Jim, 5–7, 11, 18, 19, 26–30, 34–38, 40–42, 49, 55, 60–64, 66, 67, 72–74, 77, 82, 85, 87, 109, 110, 128, 156, 157, 159, 164, 192, 201, 204
Massey, Douglas 17, 206
Maxwell, Alderman 71, 90, 93, 140
Metropolitan Police Area 23, 35
Metropolitan Police Force 2, 6, 13, 16, 23, 31, 39, 43–48, 52, 75, 104, 165
Midlands 53
Milburn, PC Tom, 68–72, 106, 200–202
Military Intelligence 49, 50
Montreal 209
Morning Post 10, 26, 51
Mussolini 138

National Bakers Strike (1919) 192
National Federation of Discharged Soldiers 205
National Industrial Conference 42
National Union of Dock Labourers 61
navy 140–143, 148, 191
Northern Ireland 13, 15
Nott-Bower, Sir William 86, 113, 121, 122
NUPPO *passim*
NUR 59, 157, 194–196, 202

O'Brien, PC Tom 103–107, 165–167, 183, 201, 202
O'Keeffe, Richard 37, 83–85, 89, 99, 100, 101, 117–119, 144–147, 150, 153, 169, 176, 180, 181, 183, 184, 189, 190, 198, 199, 200, 205, 207
Old Kent Road (London) 113, 114
Old Street (London) 108
overtime 18, 72

pay (police) 11, 17, 20, 30, 38, 40, 43, 47, 55, 56, 69, 110, 121
pensions (police) 7, 11, 38, 46, 70, 121, 127, 128, 206
Petchey, PC Leonard 37, 45, 53–60, 89, 94, 105, 106, 116, 117, 168, 195, 197, 205
pickets 86, 87, 91, 106, 111, 112
Plateau (Liverpool) 174, 197, 205
Police Act 54, 65, 66
Police and Prison Officers Journal 49, 52, 62–64
Police Bill 2, 39, 41, 43, 74, 77, 127, 136, 157, 192, 204
Police Federation 39, 74, 165
Police Review 15
Police Strike of 1919, The 17
Prime Minister *see* Lloyd George, David
Prison Officers 26, 35
'Prussian', the (Lieutenant General Sir Nevil Macready) 14, 28, 55, 165

Quebec 209

Rawlinson, MP 187
rent allowance (police) 18
Representative Board 27, 29, 31, 32, 38
Rhondda rioters 14
Riot Act 1, 151, 154, 184
rioting 145–147, 149–152, 159–163, 174–188
Ritchie, Alderman John 96–98, 100, 101, 137, 139–141, 144, 180, 191
River Police 87
Roberts, Frederick, MP 127
Roberts, George 50
Robinson, Councillor 205
Rose Hill police station (Liverpool)

213